'How do you think the
lesson went?'

'It makes no difference
what I think. You've already
made up your mind.'

How do you think the lesson went?

Blogs & Articles
2017 - 2019

Fake Headteacher

Email
headteachernewsletter@outlook.com

Web
www.headteacher-newsletter.com

Twitter & Facebook
@fakeheadteacher

Search
Teachwire

Search
Teach Primary

ISBN-13: 9798637582457

Disclaimer

Some of this book is fictitious.
It depends where you work as to how much.
If I have described your school, I am sorry. I do not work at your school. Or do I?

Contents

Introduction

Despite having a very good track record working in several primary schools, I found myself an inch away from being sacked because of an ambitious Head wanting to impress the academy chain with his non-negotiables and excessive workload policies. Some did not make it. They were forced out - or left because of the stress or could afford to quit teaching.

I sat in front of my laptop over the Christmas holiday in 2016. I had so much work to do. Not work for me - but for the management team, ready to be scrutinised days after returning after Christmas. I felt depressed. I was not coping. I was coming to the end of my three-week support plan and it didn't look good. Colleagues were telling me I was next. I was on the upper pay scale and rumour had it, SLT had been told to target upper pay scale staff.

Lesson observation feedback always started in the same manner. 'How do you think the lesson went?' I wasted so much time telling the observer how I thought it went – perfectly summarising the positives and even better ifs. I knew my stuff. I was very experienced.

I soon realised it made no difference what I thought. The lesson feedback sheet was always typed up beforehand, ready for me to sign. This was one of many reasons I started Fake Headteacher.

I started Fake Headteacher because I was frustrated with how I was being treated. I soon realised other teachers had been through similar experiences. It gave me the confidence to leave. I quit my job and started working in another primary school. I got my mojo back. I wasn't a bad teacher after all. I knew that, of course. I had never felt that vulnerable before. You doubt yourself.

I carried on writing blogs and articles to highlight some of the things I felt passionate about. I have received hundreds of personal messages from teachers sharing their own stories of woe.

Retention is still a big issue in schools. It doesn't seem to be improving but there are schools out there that seem to be moving away from excessive learning walks and scrutinies at all levels.

Hopefully, all schools will soon realise the pressure on staff has become excessive. Teachers are not prepared to sacrifice their well-being and family time in order to stay afloat anymore. Many are continuing to leave.

This book contains all of my blogs and articles I wrote between 2017-19. They follow a similar theme – workload and non-negotiables. They were written as a bit of fun but also to make others aware of some of the policies primary schools in particular, have adopted.

I would like to say thank you to Teachwire and Teach Primary for taking an interest in my blogs. It has been a pleasure writing articles for them.

Fake Headteacher

Newsletter No.1 - Welcome Back

Dear Staff,

It gives me great pleasure to welcome you back after the summer holiday. I hope you managed to find time to relax and spend time with your family. I realise this is hard to do during term time which is why I tried to restrict how many emails and text messages I sent you over the last six weeks.

Thank you to staff members who managed to email the information I needed. For those of you who didn't have time, because you were trying to have a break, please could you email me the information I need ASAP.

I know many of you wanted to pop into school over the holiday to create an exciting learning environment for the children. But as you know, the cleaners didn't want to be disturbed during the holiday which is why the school was only open yesterday for staff. The cleaners said they couldn't remember how your classrooms were set out, so they put all your furniture in the middle of the room. I hope that didn't cause you too many problems. It shouldn't have taken you too long to sort out. I hope by giving you the last hour on the inset day was enough time to sort your classrooms out.

I know the last few weeks of the summer term were extremely busy with productions, report writing and parents evenings and how this had a knock-on effect on the maths and English training we were intending to deliver.

I apologise if many of you are still confused with how to implement our new and exciting teaching programs this term due to the lack of training. In some ways, it was lucky the six weeks holiday arrived when it did, as I am sure you were able to read up on it further. I have pencilled in some extra meetings in addition to staff meetings so we can catch up with the training. I intend to carry out some learning walks in the first two weeks to see how it's all going.

I realise you probably didn't have time in the last week of term to meet up with your colleagues to plan for the autumn term. For those of you who have had to plan everything yourself, because you in a one form entry year group, don't worry, I won't expect all your planning to be completed until the third day back. I trust this will give you the quality time you need to ensure all areas of the curriculum are planned for in a creative manner.

Please could you share with parents your learning journeys this week too. I know they won't read them, and you probably want to concentrate on organising your classroom and planning your lessons, but it looks good if we do them.

I also realise that we are only back for three days in the first week, but we will have a staff meeting after work on the first teaching day. I realise we had an inset on the first day back, but we ran out of time and I have some important Ofsted information to share with you.

Also, please could you make sure your displays are up by Friday. Unfortunately, PPA won't start until week two because the teacher is sick.

Have a great few days with your new class.

PS. I forgot to mention last term that baseline testing needs to happen in the first few days. I realise you probably had lots of fun activities and get-to-know-you games to play, but this data will be good to show Ofsted.

PPS. Please make sure you regularly check your emails over the next few days, as this is how I will be communicating with you this term. I know we are a small school but emailing means I can contact you more easily.

Fake Headteacher

Newsletter No.2 - Planning Please

Dear Staff,

I trust you have had an enjoyable few weeks with your new classes. I had every intention of walking around the school this week, but I have been so busy in my office.

It would be great to see first-hand what you and the children are doing this term. Perhaps I might pop into your class after school to ask how you are and how your lessons are going? I will have to see how the week pans out.

I must remind you of the importance of typing up your weekly plans. I expect your literacy and maths planning on my desk first thing on a Monday morning and a copy to be saved on the server.

I understand this is another job to do on a Monday morning, but the plans will look good in my green folder. I probably won't look at them but at least I can access them anytime I need to. Ofsted won't want to see them either, but I would still like a copy on my desk in any case.

It's amazing that we can now save our planning on one computer at school and then access it on another computer somewhere else in the building. The school server is very smart so please save your weekly plans onto it.

I suppose you could use the same planning sheet next year but in truth, you will probably just start again. Still, I think it's a valuable use of your time to upload it to the server. I doubt I will check it's there, but I must insist that you do it - although I don't really know why.

Also, it is good practice to write down what you will say to the children for your lesson inputs and explain at length how you will deliver each lesson. It is a good idea to write down what you want your teaching assistant to do as well, just in case you get a sore throat that morning and you are unable to explain personally.

And most importantly, it is also useful to write down what resources you will need: e.g. A4 paper, felt tips and worksheets. Your day is busy enough without having to worry about the resources you will need that morning. At least if you have it all written down, you can remind yourself.

Please make sure you make it very clear on your plan who your special needs and pupil premium children are to ensure they get the support they deserve. If you like, you may wish to write their names in a different coloured font so the children can be easily recognised by Ofsted. This will provide good evidence that you are addressing their needs. At least if you have their names written on your plan, you will remember to teach them.

As professionals, I know you are fully aware of how to adjust your lessons daily for every member of your class but if you could annotate your planning to prove it, I would be very grateful.

In addition, if Ofsted do pay us a visit this term, I will give you a completely new planning format just for that day. I realise that this will cause you more anxiety on the eve of their visit because your planning will already be done. The Ofsted planning sheet will help you write up your lessons in more detail than your existing planning.

I appreciate you will want to concentrate on other things when we get the dreaded call, but the Ofsted planning sheet does look nice (it's got lots of blank text boxes on it!). They probably won't look at it, but I think it will help you with your preparation. It's a bit of peace of mind for me.

I recognise you would like more time preparing good quality resources and researching innovative ideas to teach maths and literacy but for the reasons specified above, please make sure your weekly plans are as detailed as possible. You never know, a supply teacher might have to teach your class one day and without your detailed planning, they won't know how to teach that day.

If you are ill one day, please make sure you email your planning and any resources you may have by 7am. I appreciate you might not feel like it, but supply teachers will need to have a minute-by-minute account of what you want the children to do. It would be unreasonable to ask the supply teacher to use their initiative and imagination for the one day you are out.

It is much better for them to use planning they don't really understand and for the behaviour of the children to be negatively affected rather than allowing the supply teacher to do their own thing, where they would feel more confident and have a much better day with the children.

Please make sure you spend many hours each week writing up your detailed plan. I realise that you are all professionals and given the choice, you wouldn't write such detail on your planning. I assume you would use a format that worked for you as we all work in different ways. However, we must make sure we are all working in an identical manner. I am just wondering how much time you spend looking at your planning during the week. I assume you read it all the time because you spend so long writing it.

If you have any questions about your planning, please email me.

Have a super weekend.

Fake Headteacher

Newsletter No.3 - Accountability

Dear Staff,

I hope you have had a great week. Thank you for completing the pupil progress sheets I asked for. I appreciate that you know your class very well and you understand how to move learning forward. However, I need to prove it by asking you to fill in more sheets and spend time in long meetings where you tell me how you will provide provision for the learning of your class.

I appreciate you trained hard at university to become a teacher and as a professional, you are more than capable of recognising which children need support, but it is very good practice to have pupil progress meetings several times a year just in case. I can use the sheets to prove to Ofsted that teachers at my school can identify the needs of their class.

I am very pleased that we now have a detailed scheme of work for maths and literacy. We now have consistency across the school and colleagues within each year group are teaching identical lessons. I realise that you probably came into teaching with the idea that you would be able to create fun lessons and teach in manner that you saw fit. You would bring your own personality to lessons. However, we all need to deliver the same lessons now, at the same time and in the same way.

In addition, there may be times when you feel like a robot – simply delivering lessons that the school has told you to deliver. You are correct. Please do not deviate from the school schemes of work. Do not teach lessons that you think will work better for your class or year group – especially if it doesn't fit in with your current learning journey. Remember, your books need to show a golden learning journey and I don't expect to see two days of other work that disrupts that journey.

I realise that a tornado ripped through part of our village this week, and many of you wanted to write about it in your literacy books. But I hope you understand why you weren't allowed (see notes below).

It wasn't on your topic overview for parents this week and they might complain (although in truth, they probably haven't read it in detail and won't care if you do different things).

It would disrupt the current learning journey in their books – what would Ofsted say about that?

What if your colleague doesn't want to write about the tornado? It would mean that classes within a year group might have different work in their books. So please – just teach what we tell you.

This applies to other areas of the curriculum too. For example, please follow the school policy for teaching spelling, reading, mental maths and phonics. There may be times where you might like to use different strategies that you have seen at other schools. Even though these may have helped those schools achieve accelerated progress – please don't use them here. At the end of the day, we have decided how you should be delivering lessons and you must adhere to the rules.

Following recent lesson observations, I have decided I want to see greater consistency across the school. So please make sure you have read my guidance notes below in order to accomplish this.

You must always use randomly named lolly sticks in your classrooms to ask children questions - regardless of whether you want to use them or not. If you don't use lolly sticks, the pupils' learning will suffer.

Introductions and plenaries need to look the same across the school. I appreciate you may want to do these in your own way, but I would like everyone to do these in the same manner specified in the guidance pack.

Please could everyone mark in an identical manner – as set out in the marking policy, even if you think you are writing comments that you feel have to be seen in book scrutinies – and not what you actually want to write.

Your displays must look the same across the school, even though you thought you would be able to be creative with your classroom displays when you started teaching. Our display policy will ensure children will learn well. If you disagree with our display policy because you feel we are restricting your own professional ideas, then this is unfortunate. Just stick to the policy.

With all this in mind, I must reiterate – YOU are accountable for the progress of your class. I appreciate we have stripped away any individuality and professional creativity you have to enhance the learning of your class. You may feel suffocated with so many policies to follow and teaching lesson content you have little control over.

But your data each term must look good. If it doesn't, you are fully responsible. Of course, if your data looks good, I will take the credit and I may be snapped up by an academy to become Head of several schools – turning hundreds of teachers into robots.

In addition, if your data is poor, you will not get a pay rise and you will be put onto a coaching programme that will destroy your confidence and self-esteem. You will probably want to leave teaching even though you are an amazing and dedicated teacher.

Maybe in the future, you will be trusted to teach how you like and a high stakes teaching system will be eradicated. In the meantime, teach how we say, and you will be fine. Maybe.

Fake Headteacher

Newsletter No.4 - Marking

Dear Staff,

Thank you for allowing me to look at your books this week. It was lovely to see a range of work in maths and literacy. I didn't ask for topic books because these subjects are not as important, even though I know you work just as hard to make these books look fantastic.

I asked for three books of differing abilities. This gave you plenty of time to ensure these books looked as good as possible - by adding in extra bits of marking that you didn't do at the time. Perhaps what I should do in future, is to collect a random sample of books. This would give me a better picture of who marks consistently for all pupils - rather than teachers just playing the silly book scrutiny game.

Overall, I was disappointed with the standard of marking in the books I looked at. I was alarmed to see that some books had learning objectives written by the children themselves!

Although writing the objective themself probably helps them to remember the learning objective and gives them an opportunity to use a ruler (which we all know children still struggle to use), I must insist you waste your time by typing up the learning objective for them.

I realise this must take you a long time every day because you produce them for literacy and maths (and sometimes for several ability groups in each lesson), but it is something you must do. I appreciate this is a job you usually do at home; printing them off using your own printer ink, photocopying them in the morning before trimming and sticking them in their books. But, please do them - they look good.

I overheard a member of staff say teachers would rather spend time planning lessons and preparing resources. I disagree. I feel that typing up a learning slip is good use of your time.

In addition, I was staggered to see a 'success criteria' list with only four bullet points on. Please make sure your 'success criteria' list has at least eight bullet points on. I know the children will find this overwhelming and means your learning slip will have more words on it than the child's actual work, but it looks good.

I realise that the children rarely achieve all eight bullet points, but it proves that your subject knowledge is excellent.

I was hugely disappointed to see teachers not using the marking code fully when marking their books. As you know, we agreed to use my thirty-seven codes and symbols list to mark the books.

In one class, the only marking I saw were good words and sentences ticked, and corrections or editing opportunities circled. This simply won't do. One Year 2 teacher had double ticked the following sentence even though the piece of work was about adverbs! *'Beneath the mysterious oak tree, slept a weeping wizard clutching his broken wand with his wise hands.'*

I appreciate this sentence was excellent for a Year 2 child and a double tick written on the sentence and a sticker would have made a real difference to that pupil, but it had nothing to do with the learning of the lesson - adverbs. Please do not use your professional judgement in this manner - only comment on the learning for that lesson.

In fact, the child had clearly demonstrated good use of adverbs in the same piece of work, but the teacher just wrote, *'Well done. Good use of adverbs.'* The teacher hadn't written a next step or written something for the child to improve. You *always* have to say what they should improve. You must prove you know how to improve their work.

I realise you are fully aware of what each child needs to do the next day and that you adjust your planning accordingly, but you must always tell the child what to improve. Simply writing *'Excellent work today, you must be very proud. You had a positive mind-set. Well done,'* will not be tolerated. In many ways, you don't have time to write such motivational comments, as this doesn't prove you are aware of how to extend their learning.

Staff must also use green and pink highlighters to show what is good and what can be improved. Simply ticking or commenting on a child's work will not suffice. I realise this makes marking laborious and takes away how you want to mark but please don't use your professional judgment to mark a child's piece of work.

I appreciate what you *want* to write is very different to what I *expect* you to write. It's all about making the books look good. This must be very frustrating for you, especially as you are accountable for their progress.

You probably didn't realise this when you first thought about becoming a teacher. You probably thought you could cleverly target children with personal feedback, individual marking styles and reward systems to motivate a wide range of personalities in your class. Sorry about that.

In order to prove the child has made progress under my marking guidance, please ask the children to respond to your comments in a different coloured pen. It makes no difference to the child's progress, but it looks good for Ofsted apparently. I will be looking for evidence of children responding to your marking in more depth next time. If you could then respond to their responses, before they respond again in a different colour pen, that would be great.

Can I also add that you should be 'deep marking' at least once a week. I am not sure what 'deep marking' looks like and I don't have any samples of 'deep marking' but if you could make sure you do it, I would appreciate it. I was frustrated to see teachers deciding when best to deep mark and when not to. However, you must do it once a week regardless. Again, please refer to the thirty-seven step marking code and symbol sheet for more guidance.

I was also alarmed that teachers have not been talking to their children about their learning. I only saw *'Verbal feedback given'* once across all the books I took in. I must remind you that your job requires you to talk to the children and to provide them with quality verbal feedback. I was surprised to see that teachers are not talking to their class. Please ensure you write *VF* or *verbal feedback given* if you offer advice to a child. We must prove you are talking to your class.

Thank you for your hard work as always. If you have any questions about green and pink marking, writing next steps, creating long learning slips, talking to your class, deep marking or how to respond to responses from responses from responses, please feel free to ask.

Fake Headteacher

Newsletter No.5 - Lesson Observations

Dear Staff,

We have finally made it to the end of half-term. Thank you for your hard work completing the data analysis, completing your marking, staying late for parents' evening and running parent workshops. I realise that lesson observations and learning walks didn't do anything to ease your workload but that's just the way it goes. I need to make sure you are still good teachers.

By completing learning walks and formal lesson observations I will be able to decide who needs coaching this year. I must protect myself because if Ofsted happen to see a poor lesson, I can tell them that I have already put in place an action plan for you. I know you are good teachers most of the time, but I can't afford to be caught out.

In nearly all the lessons I observed, I couldn't help noticing how untidy your working walls were. I appreciate that schools have moved away from static displays that used to look gorgeous, full of interactive questions and stimuli to engage the children, but you must now update your working walls regularly - every day if possible. They should look funky, slightly off centre and with nothing backed to show how cool and hip we are - to really prove that the working wall *really is* work in progress. Don't even think about using a staple gun - blu-tack or pin everything!

Everyone started their working walls off well but as the term's workload has increased, you have appeared to have added less and less. Sometimes they look unfinished or even out of date by two weeks. Please update them after school as much as you can. You can always mark your books and plan your lessons at home.

Remember, I only wanted to see a typical 'day to day' lesson. This gives me a good picture of how you teach. However, for those of you who surprised me with a 'one-off' special lesson, I was really impressed. I appreciate this was playing the 'lesson observation game' and the lesson had no bearing to the rest of your week, but it was worth it. For those of you who did as I asked and taught a lesson based on careful daily observations of the children, making good use of assessment for learning and daily re-grouping of children, I wasn't as pleased.

Your lessons weren't quite as snappy and were lightly resourced, which was a shame. You probably wanted to show yourself in a normal situation. You are probably more confident as a teacher and did not feel the need to rely on a special 'one-off' lesson to impress me.

Perhaps I should demand that no one teaches 'one-off' lessons for observations because they don't reflect your day to day teaching. I still want to see a normal lesson. Confused?

If I was still allowed to give lesson grades, I would certainly give outstanding to those of you who were up until three in the morning every night this week preparing for your 'one-off' lesson. I appreciate this appears to reward teachers who prioritise school over their health and important family time but that's just how it is. To be good or better, I always reward the all-singing and dancing lessons, even though I know these lessons are not typical. I know this sends the wrong message to some of you but that's just how I see it. I also tell people I only want to see normal lessons. Still confused?

I apologise for missing the first ten minutes of some lessons. I was held up in the office. I hope you didn't spend too long preparing your snappy starter to 'wow' the children and to engage them in your lesson. I appreciate this part of your lesson is where you feel more confident because it looks good and shows off your positive personality. Sorry. Similarly, I had to leave earlier than anticipated during other lessons. Sorry. I hope you didn't spend hours preparing your lesson. I always try to stay the whole hour out of respect and to show an interest in your teaching methods. After all, they do form part of your formal professional appraisal. I hope I saw the best parts of your lessons before I left.

Please make sure the children can regurgitate the learning objective. Children must know what they are learning about. If they can't tell me 'word for word' the learning objective, they are clearly not learning anything. For example, in one class children were happily playing in the role play shop where they had to add up small amounts of money and give change. When I asked the Year 2 children what they were learning about, they replied, 'We are learning how to play shops.'

As a result, the teacher has now been offered extra coaching from another teacher from another school. I know we have many good teachers in our school that could easily offer informal mentoring - which would stop the embarrassment of having a coach publicly visit them each week, but it seems quite fashionable to have 'coaches' at the moment. The shop lesson would have been excellent other than that. It was a shame the children didn't know what they were learning.

On the plus side, I enjoyed spending time with many different groups. I hope this didn't affect your lessons too much. I realised afterwards, when I read one plan properly, the group I sat with was going to be working with the TA. I am sorry about that. Perhaps I should just sit back more and observe the lesson so that you can approach any table without thinking - 'Oh no, she has sat with that group. I better go to another group.' You know me, I always seem to pick the wrong child or group to sit with and then judge your lesson on their responses.

Many of you have expressed concerns that you have had fantastic feedback for delivering the same lessons in your previous schools but rarely receive any positive feedback from me. That's because every school is different regardless of the children's learning. Most Headteachers have a particular way they want you to teach and if you don't follow their personal philosophies you won't do very well. It's probably not fair on so many levels but that's just how it is.

For example, I prefer to see an overuse of lolly sticks for questioning. If you don't use them, your feedback will suffer. I also like the learning objective shared right at the beginning, even if it means the anticipation of the lesson and the 'discovered' learning is ruined. I also like plenty of mini plenaries. I don't know why but it seems to be quite fashionable. Also, please refer to your working wall just to highlight how up to date it is. I always like children in their seats so I can easily track how the different abilities are doing. If you insist on doing drama or exciting maths lessons where the children are engaged and having fun away from their desk, please do so for just a few minutes. I don't know the children very well, so I won't be fully aware of how you are extending the learning of different abilities.

Wouldn't it be great if I made my personal teaching philosophies transparent to you, so you knew how to get better feedback? If teachers knew what I prefer to see, then I am sure they would produce better lessons.

Two of our younger teachers are beginning to understand this and they have nearly sussed out how to please me. For those of you who have been teaching at my school for some time, you already know how to pull the perfect lesson out of the bag. That's why you stay. How would your teaching be assessed if you moved school? I am looking for consistency across the school so please don't teach lessons you know might upset me, even though another Head thought your lessons were great. It shouldn't matter but it does.

Finally, it is no surprise that teachers with smaller classes, with minimal behaviour problems did very well. For those of you with very challenging classes, who had to work extra hard to find the lesson that would engage your class but not send them loopy with excitement, hard luck. Your lessons didn't look quite as good because I didn't take any of the above into consideration.

For example, in one Year 5 lesson I observed, the children stayed in their seats the whole time and produced some work. They were a little chatty but overall, there was a pleasant atmosphere. I appreciate the same class is regularly disrupted by certain individuals who think it's amusing to throw objects around, swear at each and rarely complete the work.

The class are renowned for their poor behaviour. But I still couldn't say it was a good lesson because they couldn't tell me what they were learning, and they hadn't written enough for a typical Year 5 class - despite the obvious improvement in their behaviour. Sorry.

Thank you again for allowing me to spend time in your classes this week. There were some real positives that you should be proud of. I will let you know what they are at some point. Have a great half-term and don't work too hard. I will try not to email you too often.

Fake Headteacher

Newsletter No.6 - Staff Meetings

Dear Staff,

I hope you all had a lovely half-term and didn't think about school too much. Thank you to everyone who responded to my emails and text messages. I am a workaholic and can't help myself. School is my life.

Thank you to everyone who also completed the school evaluation sheet on how efficiently our staff meetings operate. I was a little surprised with some of your comments so I would like to address your concerns in this newsletter.

Many of you said you wanted me to start staff meetings on time. We currently start about half an hour after the children leave. You said that starting fifteen minutes after the school day is ample time for people to grab a drink and have a toilet break. This would mean we would finish earlier or even on time. I disagree. I don't get out of my office often and enjoy making small talk to staff as you mingle around wondering where the staff meeting is taking place and what the agenda is. We finish school at 3:00pm so if we take our time and aim to start between 3:30pm and 4:00pm, I can talk to more people about nothing important. It doesn't matter to me what time I get home.

Someone recommended that I should be stricter about start times and ensure everyone is there promptly. I did wonder whether I should start meetings anyway and not wait for late arrivals. I suppose I could tell them off for being late afterwards. I guess it would mean we would finish on time. However, it does give me another opportunity to make even more small talk. I will think about this issue further and let you know my thoughts in a future staff meeting.

I enjoy changing the agenda each week. This way we can introduce a wider range of new policies. You can imagine my surprise when some of you reported that you feel nothing is properly embedded because I keep introducing new things. You said you would prefer to embed one initiative over consecutive meetings, rather than covering lots of policies too quickly and leaving everyone confused on how to implement them. Surely the more I introduce, the faster progress we will make.

For example, we recently discussed maths mastery, whole school spelling, safeguarding, talk for writing, assessment, whole class reading, phonics, PE, risk assessments and our new, lengthy planning formats that I don't look at. And to think we have covered all this in just three staff meetings!

I realise we will have to find more time in the year to discuss them further, but we did make some progress. Why would you want to discuss just one school improvement idea over a few weeks just so it can be thought out more carefully before moving on with something new? Again, I will consider this point and come back to it in a staff meeting in the future.

I have a very clear idea what direction I want to take the school. I will always show you that I value your opinions by asking you to spend time brainstorming ideas for a new policy. I will then thank you for your input before taking away your sheets to 'file'.

Many of you commented that this strategy devalues what you say because I simply ignore your ideas by rolling out the new policy I wrote or downloaded from Google anyway. Please understand, it would be rude of me to give you the new policy without discussion. It wouldn't appear very democratic. However, I have noted your concerns and I promise we will discuss them in a future staff meeting.

Several weeks ago, I asked the question, 'Should we blow the whistle once or twice to stop playtime?' You all looked at me blankly and I made a sarcastic comment along the lines of, 'Is anyone listening to me? Do we need more coffee?'

Apparently, some of you were offended by this remark. Some went further and explained that most of the time you don't even want to be in the staff meeting after such a long and tiring day in the classroom and yes, your concentration isn't what it could be at times. One member of staff even reported that some items we discuss are so mundane that some of you switch off.

Apparently, you are bored discussing what colour pens we write with and how much stationery we have or haven't got. Maybe I need to make more executive decisions (like the whistle on the playground) as it seems many of you don't care either way. Perhaps we can come back to this matter in another staff meeting?

I appreciate staff meetings should only last an hour (especially when you have other meetings and clubs in the week). However, because we don't get started for at least half an hour after school, you must assume they will last a lot longer. Because we are so busy, I think it's good use of our time. It's a great way to catch up with each other and bond a little.

It's lovely that many of us start talking off task which often results in laughs and giggles. Therefore, I don't mind staff meetings taking nearly two hours. However, many of you also mentioned in your evaluations that you would like me to reign in the non-essential chatting so we can make better use of the time.

Some of you said that you have families to go home to which is why you leave at 5:00pm regardless. I am uncomfortable that you feel the need to leave staff meetings earlier than everyone else. It's not fair on your colleagues who stay right to the end. Again, I will give it some thought and come back to you in another staff meeting.

I am fully aware that I have my favourite teachers and year groups. Whenever I can, I will praise them in staff meetings. You should all aspire to be like them. I understand this can make you feel bad about yourself, but I like doing it. In fact, I was glad that some of you picked up on this strategy on your evaluation sheets.

When I can, I will praise my favourites in every staff meeting. I only tend to listen to what they contribute. A member of staff said in her evaluation, 'What's the point sharing my ideas. You won't like them anyway.' I am sad about this but it's totally true. I won't discuss this matter in a future staff meeting.

Finally, can I thank you all for the additional discussions we have had at the end of our meetings. As you know, I am very relaxed about 'Any other business?' It's such a valuable use of our time going around the room, asking everyone if there's anything else they want to add.

The first Headteacher I worked for was so boring. We had to let her know before staff meetings what we wanted to discuss so she could prioritise items. She also said that 'any other business' should be restricted to reminders or quick messages and not for asking lengthy last-minute questions or handing out documents for us to look at during the week etc. I disagree with her philosophy. I am never in a rush to leave school, so I am always happy to chat about anything at the end. Your evaluation sheets suggest that you dread this additional conversation and just want to go home. We will come back to this matter in a future staff meeting.

Just to clarify, there will always be a staff meeting each week even though sometimes we don't need one. I just love having them. It was suggested that I could occasionally cancel non-essential staff meetings so you could catch up with your heavy workload. No.

Please remember next week's staff meeting is on our new initiative 'How to plan a good design and technology unit of work'. I know this isn't top priority at the moment, but we mustn't ignore the wider curriculum. We can come back to what maths mastery looks like in a future staff meeting.

If you need to discuss anything else about our staff meetings, I will be in my office pretending to look at your planning and timetables.

Fake Headteacher

Newsletter No.7 - Micro-managing

Dear Staff,

It's been another busy week at school with observations, learning walks, parents' evenings and pupil progress meetings.

My newsletter this week will attempt to address your concerns regarding micro-managing.

At the end of the day, the buck stops with me. If Ofsted puts us into requires improvement or special measures, it will ruin my reputation. Because I have now been at the school for over a year, I will no longer be able to blame my predecessor. In order to prevent this, I will micro-manage you as best I can by removing any professional freedom you may wish to exercise.

First, I will use my 25-point book scrutiny checklist to ensure you are using the correct pens and learning slips etc. In the past, I used to look at progress in your books, regardless of what colour pens you used or how well you 'deep marked'. Progress is something I care less about now. I am now looking for consistency. I need to see pink and green highlighting, purple pen evidence, long learning slips, children responding to your feedback, short or long dates etc. I appreciate this puts extra pressure on you, but it means consistency is adhered to.

I expect learning objectives to be shared at the beginning of your lesson, tool kits created, and success criteria shared. If this doesn't occur, it means your lessons are boring and learning does not take place. I also expect you to refer to your learning objective throughout your lesson in mini plenaries. Children must be able to regurgitate their learning objective word for word otherwise they will not have a clue what they are learning about.

You must give children opportunities to work in random pairs, mixed ability pairs and ability groups in the same lesson. You must use talk partners or learning buddies. You mustn't allow children to put their hands up. Use random lolly sticks to choose children to answer questions even though you want to direct questions at particular children. If you don't apply any one of these strategies, because it's not appropriate for the lesson, I will suggest it is something you do next time.

More able children must never be allowed to consolidate their learning. You must show me how you always push their learning forward. Your pupil premium children must be mentioned on your planning and you or your TA must support them in the lesson even though there are other children who need your support more.

Your TA must not support your SEN children. I will accuse you of not allowing them to work independently. Sometimes, I will criticise you for butterfly teaching (moving from table to table - looking for opportunities to extend or support children within the lesson). Then, on another day, I will criticise you for only working with one focus group and not being aware what the rest of the class are doing.

Children must provide peer support in your lessons. Please ask them to criticise their partner's work and write next steps in their friend's book despite the fact some children are not comfortable having another child read through and write on their work. I am sure you would be very comfortable asking a random member of staff to read your class reports and comment on how well you have written them.

In addition, I will expect children to always use mini whiteboards in lessons. I like whiteboards. Children must be able to explain their thinking. If they can't, I doubt they have learnt anything. Children who shout out 'Yes, I get it now,' will always prove that child has made good progress. Quiet children, who are not as vocal, probably haven't made progress.

Your lesson must be pacey, full of humour and all children must make accelerated progress. You must use the new resources I bought for the school even if you don't like them or feel other resources would work better. Your lesson feedback will suffer if you don't use my expensive new resources.

You must take plenty of photos during your lessons and spend lunchtime downloading, printing and sticking them into books - just to show me and prove some of the activities they have engaged in. I appreciate this is time consuming, but it provides good evidence. For example, when children make pizza, take a photo to prove it. But remember please don't use the colour photocopy to provide exciting learning resources. We can't afford it.

You must never teach content from the year above. For example, if a pupil can count in 2s, 5s and 10s in Year 2, never teach them how to count in 3s, 4s or 8s (Year 3). You must discourage children to write in paragraphs if the curriculum doesn't require it for your year group.

I was very surprised to see one pupil being shown how to use adverbs in their writing, but they weren't required to learn it yet. Don't do it. Hold your children back. This will ensure everything in Year 6 will be completely new and they will have to work hard to cram it all in before SATs. I suppose it would make more sense for some of our Year 5s to already know some of the Year 6 curriculum before they get there. Perhaps it will be less stressful for the children? I get mastery. I really do. But hold them back at all costs.

Your displays must be working walls with very few static displays. Working walls must be updated regularly and look similar from class to class.

So, you see, I must micro-manage everyone. I need all my staff to be clones. My philosophy is the only way. If you choose not to follow my philosophy, your data and appraisals will suffer. Your teaching will suffer. Of course, if your data is still poor - even though you have strictly followed my policies, I will blame you anyway.

You may at times feel suffocated with so many hoops to jump through. You may not enjoy your job anymore because you don't have the freedom to teach and mark in a manner you see fit. You may feel that no one trusts you and a *'we must improve'* culture is wearing you down. You are correct.

Fake Headteacher

Newsletter No.8 - Maths

Dear Staff,

Thank you for your recent letter regarding book scrutinies. I read it very carefully and disagreed with most of it. I am sorry. We will come back to it at some point in a future staff meeting.

As you know, I now have several maths systems in place for you to fully implement. I would like to reiterate how important it is to be very familiar with:

- Our new purchased scheme of work for maths
- Our new tracking system *(that is not related to our new scheme of work)*
- 'What mastery looks like' documents *(that are not related to our new scheme of work)*
- Our formal written tests I found online *(that are not related to our new scheme of work)*

We are so lucky to be teaching in a climate where we can tap into so many super resources. Our new maths scheme is amazing. It cost over £5,000 so you definitely need to use it otherwise the governors will give me a hard time.

I expect to see the new resources out on display. The governors will be doing a learning walk soon to observe how the children are using the resources enthusiastically in lessons. Perhaps they were before?

I know the scheme works because my last school used it ten years ago, and my friend recommended it. You will need to follow the long and medium-term plans for this scheme regardless of whether you think you could do a better job. You will be accountable for the data in any case so I can't lose. If the data is good, it will be down to me and if it's disappointing, I will put you on a coaching program and freeze your pay.

In addition, please make sure you update the children's progress on our new tracking system written by people who are making a lot of money out of it and seemingly, by looking at some of the statements, have never stepped foot in a classroom.

The tracking system doesn't complement our maths scheme so you may find it problematic matching objectives. You will probably spend two weeks teaching a unit from our new scheme only to find you can't meet a particular objective on our new tracking program because they are different. Weird eh! That's because it's all down to interpretation of the new curriculum. Still, it's nice to have the two side by side.

As well as your teacher assessments, please could your children complete a formal written maths test every half-term. It doesn't completely match up with the maths scheme of work or the tracking program, but it will give us more data if we need it.

I realise you haven't taught most of the content covered in the tests (because it doesn't relate to our other systems), but I am sure the children will do great. I expect them to do well. If you could bring the test data to your next pupil progress meeting, I would appreciate that. I might use it. I might not. I might just look in their books. Or, I might look at the tracking data. Who knows?

Isn't it great that our new tracking program has so many objectives! It means the children will learn so much more. For example, in Year 4, there are 72 objectives to meet for maths. It will cleverly work out how many objectives a child has met or nearly met and tell you how each child is doing. I have no idea how this is calculated so you will have to guess which children will meet expectations at the end of the year.

If these predictions are wrong, I will conclude that you are incompetent, and you don't know your children. With 72 objectives to tick off red, orange, yellow, blue, purple, beige, black, yellow etc, you should find teaching maths mastery very easy.

Maths mastery is great because it means you can dive deeper and deeper into children's understanding of maths. With 96 objectives to meet in Year 5 this should be easy. With two days to meet each objective, this should be achievable even if they are already two years behind where they should be.

You must never say a child has met an objective unless they prove it several times over and in a problem-solving situation. For example, our new tracking program for Year 3 says, 'I can count in 4s and 8s.' If they can count in 4s and 8s, you must not tick it green to say they have met it. You will have to wait a few weeks so it is away from the point of teaching (even if they knew it already and you didn't need to teach it) and then give them a ridiculous and weird problem to solve just to prove they can count in 4s and 8s - again. Mmm. I think that makes sense. I appreciate this is irritating because you know they have met the objective really.

Also, your colleagues will be suspicious that you have already met some objectives. Play the game. Slowly show progress over time. This way you won't attract any unwanted attention. Try not to tick 'exceeding' for anything because colleagues won't like it and your judgements will be secretly disputed. Play safe. As Goldilocks once said, 'Not too cold and not too hot.'

As well as implementing our new maths scheme, our new tracking system and our new testing regime, can you also teach from the 'What mastery looks like' documents because everyone seems to be using it. It has excellent examples of fluency, reasoning and problem solving. It's a shame we have other systems in place now.

However, I am sure you will happily spend hours looking at our new planning and assessment resources and somehow merge the content to ensure the children can do all of it. I am not sure which of these resources are important yet and what data I will be judging you from, so just do your best. You will be accountable for all of it.

Fake Headteacher

Newsletter No.9 - Reading

Dear Staff,

I will be focusing on Year 6 reading over the next few weeks. As you know, our online objective statements focus on the children having 'positive attitudes' so if they seem to be smiling then you *must* 'meet' their objectives (see below).

If they are shy or don't appear to be enjoying reading, *do not* tick 'met' even though they understand the text. The objectives are very clear - 'they must have a positive attitude'.

Our school data program requires you to collect evidence for 21 reading objectives. The weighting for each one is equally spread. However, the SATs paper is weighted differently. For example, 15% of our school reading objectives focus on *'word meaning, retrieval and inference'* compared to around 80% on the SATs paper.

So, do you spend more time teaching *'word meaning, retrieval and inference'* to ensure a good SATs score or do you thinly spread your teaching to cover the school's 21 objectives to make your TA data look good?

You can't really win. Some of our school objectives are perfectly vague so do your best to collect evidence for them. I have listed a few below with some guidance to help you along your way.

Maintain positive attitudes to reading by reading and discussing an increasingly wide range of fiction, poetry, plays, non-fiction and reference books or textbooks.

Our non-fiction and poetry books in school are over ten years old. We have a few reference books in the library, but someone said the children now use the 'google' book. I haven't seen it in the library. I must look out for it. Do the best you can.

Maintain positive attitudes to reading by increasing their familiarity with a wide range of books, including myths, legends and traditional stories, modern fiction, fiction from our literary heritage, and books from other cultures and traditions.

I am not sure if we have these books in school - certainly not enough for everyone to access properly. Make sure children have positive attitudes towards the books we do have and then *you can* tick 'met'.

Maintain positive attitudes to reading by preparing poems and plays to read aloud and to perform, showing understanding through intonation, tone and volume so that the meaning is clear to an audience.

If a child doesn't use their voice correctly then you must assume they have no understanding of the poem so, *do not* tick 'met'. If they understand the poem but seem to have a negative attitude, then *do not* tick 'met'.

If they seem to be enjoying the book because they are reading for pleasure, *do not* tick 'met'. They must regularly ask themselves questions to maintain their positive attitude. Assess this somehow.

Maintain positive attitudes to reading by summarising the main ideas drawn from more than one paragraph, identifying key details that support the main ideas.

You only get 0-3 marks for this in the SATs so don't bother with this one.

Maintain positive attitudes to reading by drawing inferences such as inferring characters' feelings, thoughts and motives from their actions and justifying inferences with evidence.

This is a huge part of the SATs test but bizarrely it only counts for 5% of our school data. As long as they have a positive attitude by justifying their answers that's all that counts. If they don't have a positive attitude, then please *do not* tick 'met'.

Maintain positive attitudes to reading by recommending books that they have read to their peers, giving reasons for their choices.

If a child doesn't want to recommend a book with a positive attitude they obviously can't read. You better put them back on the phonics program. If children in Year 3 can recommend a book with a smile, then feel free to tick the Year 6 objective as 'met' in advance.

Maintain positive attitudes to reading by participating in discussions about books that are read to them and those they can read for themselves, building on their own and others' ideas and challenging views courteously.

You must judge a children's ability to read by how polite they are. Please *do not* tick 'met' if they are reluctant to join in discussions or forget to say thank you. Again, if you think a Year 3 child is polite when discussing a book, please go ahead and tick the Year 6 objective for them in advance.

Maintain positive attitudes to reading by explaining what they have read, including through formal presentations and debates, maintaining a focus on the topic and using notes where necessary.

Any child who isn't comfortable delivering presentations *must not* meet this objective. They must be jolly and confident in order to show they understand the text.

Maintain positive attitudes to reading by predicting what might happen from details stated and implied.

You only get 0-3 marks for this in the SATs so don't bother with this one too. However, if they predict something might happen with a big smile then *you must* tick 'met'.

You must collect evidence for your class all the time to prove that a child understands the text. I appreciate collecting reading evidence is hard, but it must be done. Maybe one day you will be trusted to make a judgement without the need to write a full commentary of what they said.

In addition, can I remind you to film each child reading each term. I saw one school do it and I really like it. I have no idea why they do it because I can't imagine they watch the films back. I suppose you could see if their fluency had improved but you could always just tell me. I trust you. Oh, hang on. No. Film the children every term.

Good luck with your class reading. I have no idea if we are supposed to be teaching whole class reading or group reading at the moment. I will let you know when I have time to think about it.

Fake Headteacher

Newsletter No.10 - Writing

Dear Staff,

Thank you for updating your writing objectives on our school tracking software that no one really understands.

I have to say how extremely pleased I was with some of the data. In particular, I would like to bring to your attention the outstanding hot task assessment written by Josh in Year 3. He managed to hit nearly every objective on our tracking program. I am confident he will meet the end of year objectives.

<u>The Haunted House</u>

Tom went **slowly** into the haunted house after his **grammar** lesson   he ate a **potato although** he wasn't hungry. He felt **great**. He wished he had **grated** his cheese so he could have it with his **potato**   Tom hoped to see a **submarine** in the house. He remembered learning about them in a **comprehension** lesson once   The **boys'** toys were in the corner of the room. They always **misbehave** in class. He noticed a **calendar above** the table. Tom thought it was **an untidy** house   he was **disappointed** so he went the **supermarket** instead. 'I am off'

Spell further homophones ✔

Spell words that are often misspelt ✔

Place the possessive apostrophe accurately in words with regular plurals ✔

Use further prefixes and suffixes and understand how to add them ✔

Form nouns using prefixes (super-, anti-) ✔

Use conjunctions, adverbs and prepositions ✔

Use the correct form of 'a' or 'an' ✔

Inverted commas to punctuate direct speech ✔

It would have been better if he had used capital letters and full stops in the right place, but it doesn't come up on the Year 3 tracking program so don't worry about it.

Perhaps some amazing adjectives would have added more interest. Or maybe he could have varied his sentence length to create tension. Also, he could have used a range of punctuation marks such as ! ( ) ? ... - ; but again, there is no need to tick these on the Year 3 tracking program, so don't bother teaching it.

Please don't teach children objectives that are in the year above (we are trying to emulate the maths mastery approach).

Many of you have said how frustrated you were with some of your writing tasks because, despite being very good, you were not able to tick off many objectives from the Year 3 list (because they are too narrow and boring, mostly focusing on spelling). Sorry, but you must show progress on the tracking system by ticking off the above.

Don't worry about the impact your writing has on the reader anymore or the composition generally. As long as you can tick off the year objectives to show good progress, I will be very happy.

One teacher I spoke to this week was in tears after her class had written some terrific instructions on how to look after a dragon. She had taught them how to use brackets effectively for additional information. They had also written very amusing introductions and used some short, sharp sentences for effect. The impact on the reader was excellent.

However, when she went to update her data on her tracking system, she struggled to find anything she could tick off. I have now told her to use the model text above in future (The Haunted House). She hasn't stopped crying. I can't think why.

Fake Headteacher

Newsletter No.11 - Behaviour

Dear Staff,

It's been a while since I have written a newsletter. I have been very busy downloading school policies that I have simply added our school name to and passed them off as my own.

I would like to address some of the behaviour problems we no longer have in our school.

We used to have behaviour issues but since I introduced my complicated behaviour flow chart, children are no longer sent to my room. The twenty-five page document can be found on the server. Please remember, if you can't control extreme behaviour daily, I will put you on a coaching program.

If you send me a child because you need a break from the disruption and urgently require me to give them a rollicking, I will simply send them back after ten minutes. I'm sure you understand how busy I am. However, if my iPad is charged, I will let them play on that. It's easier.

Remember, the first rule of dealing with bad behaviour is: We don't talk about bad behaviour.

You don't have time to nurture children in the same way you used to. You could afford to spend time concentrating on their social skills - often realising it was more important to focus on their social skills before tackling academic progress. However, with regular pupil progress meetings, you must now show that *all* children are making good academic progress.

I appreciate many children arrive at school already stressed due to poor parenting (not providing proper breakfast, not listening to them read, always arguing, no PE kit etc.), but this should not make any difference. The parallel class, with very supportive parents will make good progress. Your class will make the same progress. A stressful home environment does not make a difference to pupils' mind-set. Well that's I what I keep getting told.

If you must regularly take your class to the library because you have to leave a child behind to be restrained, or because they are being very disruptive, it must not affect your data. Your data still has to be very good. I realise, due to lack of funds, we can't replace your TA but I repeat, your data must be very good still. Perhaps you could make your lessons more exciting?

If your current class did not make enough progress the previous year, due to very poor behaviour that I know nothing about because you're too scared to tell me, you must make up the progress. Please catch up and move them forward even further so they reach expected progress.

Please ensure any children who are behind miss out on their favourite lessons in the afternoon such as music, art, history, PE etc. Put them in a variety of intervention groups. This will inspire the children even further and I am sure it will not fuel their resentment towards school in any way. I am sure they will understand, and it will help to reduce their stress levels.

Last week a member of staff claimed that although her class data looked poor, her class had made excellent progress. I was flabbergasted with this statement.

She claimed that her class now come in after break peacefully, ready to learn. Apparently, nobody storms out of class mid-lesson, slamming doors in the process.

She said that children now positively attempt some work rather than refuse to have a go. She claimed that her class are proud of their handwriting now after spending time every day focusing on it.

She spent every afternoon following a social skills program to help children learn to tolerate their differences and show respect to one another. She claimed this was good progress. It took time, but she thought it was worth it.

I disagree. Our online tracking software says differently. They still don't know what subordinating conjunctions are or how to use fronted adverbials. This is not good enough.

Just to remind you, pupil progress meetings are next week. Prove to me you know where your children are and how to help them make double the progress necessary to keep the pressure off me.

Remember, the first rule of dealing with bad behaviour is: We don't talk about bad behaviour.

Fake Headteacher

Newsletter No.12 – Report Writing

Dear Staff,

Just a reminder that your reports were due in last Monday. So far, I have only received four sets. I appreciate I emailed the new report template three weeks late and that only left you two weeks to write them (including half-term), but I think this was enough time to write them on top of your stressful workload.

I am very proud of my new report template. You will have noticed that each report is now six pages long – nearly double the length of last year. To make it easier, I have added a tick chart for core subjects to show how pupils are progressing etc. This is more than enough to tell a parent about their child's effort and attainment, but please could you also write a lengthy comment repeating the same information already highlighted in the tick chart. You will probably feel you are saying the same thing but that's alright. I am sure it won't take long.

I was surprised that many of you claim it takes between 20-40 hours to write a set of reports. With my new changes to the template, you should be able to complete them in one weekend. After all, each report is only 1,000 words. You all wrote a dissertation at University so you should find it easy to cope with the extra workload. I am sure your family won't mind. You could start them at 9pm every night for a few hours. Don't forget, you can also spend weekends writing them too. For those of you who have your own children, put films on for them so you can work. Even better, get your partner to look after them all day.

Just remember, parents will appreciate your dedication and understand the personal sacrifices you make to write them. They will read the report repeatedly and write a long comment back to you on the parent comment slip.

They will appreciate your effort and thank you multiple times over subsequent weeks. Although last year, we only received one comment slip back, which was disappointing. Hopefully with the new lengthy report, we might get a few more back this year.

I know many of you have worked hard to create a positive mind-set culture in your classroom – especially with your more challenging and vulnerable pupils. However, please make sure you make it very clear that many of them are 'working below national standards' at the top of each comment box. This will boost their self-esteem and motivate them to work harder next time. They have probably worked their socks off for you and have made excellent progress. Still, make sure they realise they are not as bright as the rest of the country.

Many of you have pupils whose behaviour can be extreme with unsupportive parents. However, to avoid further problems with parents, make sure you find lots of positives to write in the report. Twist comments so they are ambiguous and can be read positively if needed. It will probably take you hours composing these comments but it's worth it. I want all parents to be happy. Happy reports equal happy Ofsted parent comments.

Please don't copy and paste. If you do, only do it once or twice. What if a parent reads another child's report? I know your pupils attend the same lessons all year and make the same progress generally but somehow, write a completely different comment. It should almost read like they are in different classes. Parent won't understand that the same comment for handwriting, for multiple pupils, is fine. However, don't risk it.

Many of you claim writing reports leaves you exhausted and very stressed because of the time and effort it demands. However, there is absolutely no excuse to make the odd mistake. For example, he instead of she, his instead of her etc. Please proofread your reports over and over again. I know it takes hours and it is painstakingly boring, but you must find time.

Also, once you have completed your reports, you will need to spend a few more hours adjusting all the text boxes because they have moved. I didn't know how to 'fix' them so they will move all over the place. Sorry. Then spend hours changing the font size to fit inside the boxes. Then change the spelling mistake I made on one of the subheadings. Sorry.

Once I have read your reports, I will give them back to you to re-write. I am quite particular about how I want them written. I have particular grammatical bug bears. I probably should have given you one I wrote myself, so you get a feel for how I want them written. Sorry. But I am sure you can find time to re-write them days before they are due to go out.

During lesson observation week, starting next Monday, could you find time for children to write their own report comment. Please mark them and ask them to write them up neatly multiple times because they will make mistakes. If you are lucky enough to have a TA, ask them to photocopy the comments onto the reports. It's good to have written evidence that your class have enjoyed their year. Please remove any negative comments regardless of how honest they are.

Pupils love writing report comments. It's a bit like how excited you feel when you have to complete an evaluation form at the end of a course. You love it. Pupils love it too. Just be aware that they often contradict what you have already said. For example, last year many of you wrote 'They enjoyed the Romans topic'. But on their comment slip, they said 'I thought the Roman topic was boring.'

I am surprised that you all seem very stressed and on your knees at the moment. Surely report writing can't be that bad. I am sure your planning, marking and outstanding lessons have continued to take place during report writing time? I am sure your lessons have not been affected. This is why I am carrying out lesson observations next week.

For those of you who have handed in your reports on time, please check your pigeon holes where you will find your returned, annotated reports for you to amend. For those of you who have not completed them on time because of family commitments, I will be on your case this week.

After you have handed in your reports and they have been given out to parents, I might thank you for working so very hard. I might not. I usually forget.

Fake Headteacher

Newsletter No.13 - LO Slips

Dear Staff,

I trust you had an enjoyable summer break. I am re-sending this newsletter as many of you did not receive it. I did check my sent box and it was definitely posted on the 14th August. Perhaps the server wasn't working that week because nobody replied.

I would like to reiterate how important it is to type, print, trim and stick learning objective slips into pupils' books. I realise this takes up a lot of your time (especially if you are doing them for several lessons a day). But, with Ofsted just around the corner, we need to prove that staff and children have a good understanding of what they are teaching and learning.

Can you imagine a child writing a learning objective, but an Ofsted inspector was not able to read it clearly? That would be disastrous. That would prove that the pupil did not know what they were learning. It would suggest that the lesson was a complete shambles. A beautifully typed up leaning slip will prevent any misunderstanding.

It's a complete waste of time asking children to write the learning objective and date in their book. That's 2-3 minutes of every lesson wasted.

It's not as if they would start to learn what a title is or even how to use a ruler properly. It's not as though you could use this time to reinforce handwriting patterns as they write it. It's not as though you could ask them to write the learning objective straight away as a way of settling the class quickly and quietly. It's not as though it would help children to take more ownership of their work.

I understand that some of you are concerned with the amount of paper we are getting through every week. A school in the locality are now using stickers to print learning objectives on. I love the idea but it's costing them a small fortune. I am more than happy that we get through five reams of paper every week printing off learning objective slips. Although, I am nervously waiting for the Eco Warriors club to spot the waste. So far, so good!

Because you are spending so much time typing up the learning objective slips, I have noticed how fancy they are becoming. Sometimes, they are longer than the work the children produce with many 'I can...' statements to prove to Ofsted the teacher knew what to teach. Some slips I saw last term, had fancy smiley faces on too so the children could colour in the one that best depicted how they felt about their learning. I love it!

I assume the teacher considers what colour face the child draws when they are marking? Do you use a special mark book? Make sure you allow plenty of time for children to do this at the end of the lesson. Don't worry about a plenary anymore. Perhaps many of you don't require coloured faces because you already know within the lesson who is struggling or cruising and intervene appropriately?

Some slips I have seen have room for peer review comments. Genius. The longer the learning objective slip, the better. I love peer review comments. In fact, I am thinking of asking you all to read each other's class reports and provide written feedback to each other. Imagine how that would make you feel. This must be how some children feel? Especially when they are working in random pairs.

I had a frank conversation with a member of staff last term after she claimed learning objective slips are the bane of her life because they have a huge impact on her workload. She said it was all for show and teachers were quite capable of sharing success criteria and learning objectives without them.

She added that a simple title could be written by the child very quickly rather than the teacher producing learning objective slips - time saved that could be spent preparing lessons. She said instead of the teacher typing up the following...

I am learning what adverbial phrases are and how to use them at the beginning of a sentence to create interest. (with a long success criterion etc.)

The child independently writes...

Adverbial Phrases (they don't even write LO)

But how would Ofsted know the finer details of learning that took place? Our colleague argued that the children knew exactly how and why they were learning about adverbial phrases. She said this is why we use working walls - to put up success criteria and toolkits as you go.

Apparently, she claimed that it is perfectly clear what the children are doing in their books without a long learning slip to prove it. 'If you don't know they have written an introduction for a recipe with the title *Recipe Introduction* then you need your eyes tested,' she continued. I have now put her on a support plan.

When an Ofsted inspector sits next to a pupil and asks the dreaded question, 'What are you learning about?' the child will not be able to answer if a learning objective slip has not been typed up and printed. Our colleague clearly didn't understand this. The pupil will freeze and not be able to tell them. This is why I insist on learning slips being used. In fact, I encourage children to regurgitate the exact wording on the slips (in a proud Hermione Granger manner) to prove what they are learning.

No. I am sorry, but lengthy learning objective slips that take up so much of your time each week to produce, are here to stay. We have all got to show how we are impacting on learning and this is one sure way of doing it. It's all about the books people.

See you all on Monday.

Fake Headteacher

Newsletter No.14 - Working Walls

Dear Staff,

I will get straight to the point. I found time to walk around the school today to check up on you - I mean to engage with the children and show an interest in the exciting learning that is happening in classrooms.

I was very disappointed to find around 70% of display boards were still empty. We are now a few weeks into term, and you should be completely on top of your displays.

I realise in the past you would put up complete displays to excite and engage the children as soon as they entered the classroom. I appreciate you used to take pride in your topic display about dinosaurs - full of questions, information and pictures to motivate and inspire. You used to make your writing display look amazing with lots of words, punctuation ideas and good examples of quality sentences. Your displays used to be mostly static, but you changed them once a term or so.

You didn't have to update them every day or every week because you wanted to focus more on planning super lessons. Children used to regularly publish their work and you made sure their work went up on the wall. They were mounted and the children loved it! They used to feel proud and your classroom looked amazing.

You could even choose what displays to put up depending on your class. It was part of the fun. You used to love the freedom and creativity to create an amazing learning space for you pupils to work in.

But things have changed. Now I tell you what your classroom should look like. Working walls are all the fashion now. They look good for Ofsted. They make it very clear that the teacher and the children are following a well-planned learning journey. They try to prove that the learning is fun, raw, edgy, creative, full of pace and energy etc.

Nothing is mounted and most of what I expect to see now are scribbles on rough paper. Easel paper is the best. Most of the writing is too small for children to see. If you have time, you might refer to the working wall but mostly, you just crack on with the lesson.

The best working walls are the ones where paper is overlapping the borders, and everything is stuck on at funny angles.

Remember, I expect working walls for spelling, writing, maths, topic and science. Your classroom should be bare when the children start the term. I realise this is boring but if you update your working walls every day they will soon be filled.

It will take about four weeks for your working walls to be complete. Then I expect you to start all over again. Which is why I am concerned because most of your working walls are still fairly empty. You must find more time.

I have added working walls to my non-negotiables list so when I carry out my conformance walk - I mean a learning walk, I can put pressure on you later.

Good luck.

Fake Headteacher

Newsletter No.15 - New Management

Dear Staff,

As you know, an academy chain that is too big for its boots, took over the school in September and sacked the previous Fake Headteacher. I am sorry there wasn't a chance for the parents, teachers or children to say goodbye.

As you know, I have implemented a lot of changes since I was headhunted by the academy and placed in your school. They knew I had a reputation of destroying the morale of the staff. I am slowly moving up the ranks in the academy chain. I won't be here long as I expect to be an academy director soon, overseeing several schools at once and enjoying £150k a year for the privilege.

The previous management focused too heavily on developing positive relationships with difficult parents and nurturing challenging pupils and not enough attention providing all day booster groups to improve the SATs scores. I have been informed that this is something I need to change.

A few weeks ago, I carried out a mocksted. I understand you resented this - especially as Ofsted do not recommend them. However, I needed to do it so I can prove my impact over time. I appreciate many of you were upset when I graded every lesson inadequate even though most of you have a history of good to outstanding teaching. Don't worry because I said at the time, 25% of you would be good by Christmas. I am pleased to say that 25% of you are now good. By Easter, 50% of you will be good teachers again. Hopefully, you'll be one of the lucky ones. If not, I will put you on a coaching program.

The academy is very pleased with me. I know you are still very upset with how transparent these 'proof of impact' tactics seem to be but that's how it is. You must remember that the academy is in

Requires Improvement too so we must show we are making good progress by improving the standards of teaching and learning.

Many of you resented being sent to other schools to watch teachers teach lessons that were not particularly special. But at least I can tick a box to show what strategies I have put in place to help you all improve. I apologise you had to spend two hours travelling to the school - it was the nearest school in the academy chain. We don't have anything to do with our local authority schools now.

I also understand that many of you despise typing up daily A4 planning sheets for every lesson - each with three learning objectives. You said you felt like a student teacher again and felt patronised. You often complain about the excessive workload now being placed on you. But please understand it's the best way I can prove my impact. It's a very easy strategy for me to administer at your expense. Sorry.

Your lessons still need to be taught in the academy approved manner. It's just an academy thing. One model fits all 345 schools, staff and pupils. It can feel a bit regimented, with very little room for creativity and originality but it's the only way. Sorry.

Book scrutinies will continue every week. I will use a long checklist to criticise your ability to teach. Progress over time will not be on my list. Instead, I will be looking for things I can easily measure such as typed up learning objective slips, use of highlighters and purple pens, regular next steps seen, peer comments etc. I am too scared to scrap the excessive marking policy to a more effective and less time-consuming feedback policy that involves less marking. The list is too long to include here but I have stuck it to your white board so you can refer to it.

My weekly learning walks have proved extremely popular with the academy as they provide me justification for implementing more policies and non-negotiables. They are a great way to prove my impact. I will pick holes in lots of things.

Anybody on the upper pay scale should be warned. You will be on coaching programs first. The academy simply can't afford you anymore. It's much better if we weigh you down with excessive responsibilities with no time to carry them out. The aim is for you to burn out. Your well-being will be affected, and you will hopefully leave. The academy is extremely keen for me to employ five new teachers this year. I can use the academy working model to mould them. They won't know any different. Genius.

As you are aware, due to the scrapping of Year 6 foundation subjects, excessive lunchtime and after school booster groups and two hours of daily homework, our SATs results will almost certainly improve. The academy doesn't really care about the mental health of the children or staff. They only care about the data. They are under so much pressure. All being well, I will not be here in two years, so it doesn't really bother me.

Kind regards,

Fake Headteacher

Newsletter No.16 - Pupil Letter

Dear Staff,

Thank you so much for your hard work this term.

A letter was anonymously left on my desk this week. It was from a pupil who is very concerned about the teachers. I doubt for one minute the content is accurate as the pupils and staff at school are very happy. If you find out who may have written this nonsense, please let me know immediately and an investigation will be initiated.

Dear Teachers,

Why are you so tired?

Your body language suggests you are fed up. It's almost like you have to work extra hours each week without pay. But your job should be so rewarding. I don't understand. It must be easy for you to manage your workload. It's not as though you have to jump through a ridiculous set of hoops to prove your impact. Or do you?

Let me give you some tips to ease your stress.

You do not need to highlight my work with pink and green. Just tick the good bits as you read it and tell me how to improve. It's so much quicker. I take a lot pride in my work, so I don't like it when you highlight over half of my work. It ruins it. I don't mind if you circle a few things for me to check like spellings or punctuation errors. But most of the time, you can just give me verbal feedback. It's more personal and will save you hours writing comments just to satisfy a book scrutiny checklist.

Do you have to write comments every day or deep mark once a week? Who tells you to do this? Can't you decide for yourself how you give feedback? Surely, if progress is made, you have done your job.

Verbal feedback stamper or VF initials. Why do you have to prove you have spoken to me in lessons? Why do you need to prove you helped me? This seems a complete waste of your time. Please stop it. I would rather you concentrated on more important things.

I don't understand why you spend hours typing up learning objective slips. This must really annoy you. Why do you do it? Are you told to? Can't we just write a short title? You clearly know what we are learning about and you tell us every day in lessons. It seems daft that you have to do this, and it wastes so much paper. I would rather you spent the time on other important matters.

Writing two stars and a wish most days is silly. I work really hard to show I understand what you are teaching. Just give me a sticker or a house point if I do well. Why do you feel the need to write a next step all the time? It feels like you are always criticising me. It seems like my work is never quite good enough and it affects my self-esteem. If I do what you ask, just praise me. Surely my next step is the next lesson you are teaching.

Often, it feels like you are rushing through my learning. Are you under so much pressure to show progress? You are always giving me targets to achieve. You surely know what I need to do to improve. Do you have to constantly tell me? Is this a whole school thing? It puts pressure on me all the time. I just want to work hard in lessons and do my best without fear of failure.

One of the most annoying things you ask us to do is to write comments about other pupils' work. Surely you are the teacher. Isn't that your job? You make us sit in random pairs then ask us to write comments on our partner's work. You call this pupil voice or peer review. We don't like it. I don't want a pupil, who I don't like particularly, writing in my book, telling me how to improve. I am happy to read my work to my friend and celebrate my successes.

I don't really care what my friend thinks I can improve. You are the most important person who I want to impress. You tell me.

Why do you insist I write down how I feel about my learning? You often get me to colour in a smiley face or traffic light my emotions. Or even worse, I must write a sentence. It's really boring. Have you not been on a course where you are asked to fill in a course evaluation form? You don't like it do you? Well, stop asking us to review our learning every lesson.

Can't you tell how we did in our lesson? Isn't it obvious if I understand or need more help? Isn't that your job? Is pupil voice something you are encouraged to implement? Is it something a book scrutiny checklist requires? We used to discuss our work or play games at the end of the lessons. This was much more fun. Sometimes, we would read our work out!

When the Head comes in to observe us (although it's obvious he is observing you), you get over-enthusiastic. You talk a lot more than normal and seem to do mini plenaries all the time. You don't normally do this. Actually, you seem to do a lot of things you don't normally do. Does the Head have a checklist of things they are looking for?

After these observed lessons, you seem so tired for the rest of the day. Do you spend hours preparing for these special lessons? It seems like you are up all night preparing them. You suddenly produce these amazing resources that we never normally use. Surely, the Head would want to see a typical lesson. You are a great teacher. You can see how much progress we have made in our books. Why do they insist with these observations? Don't they trust you or something?

In parents' evening you used to tell my parents how I had settled into class and said nice things to boost my confidence. You might have suggested something to do at home to help me. Now you tell my parents in October that I will not be meeting expected standards for my age in nine months' time and tell them you are putting me into intervention groups. Why do you do this? Are you under pressure to show progress? Are you told to do this? I don't like it. How will you know if I will meet expected progress? What would happen if you didn't tell me or my parents this information? Would it affect my learning? It's an odd way to motivate the pupils. Surely, there is another way.

Lastly, please go back to putting our lovely work on display. We used to love seeing our writing and artwork on the wall. The classroom looked lovely and we felt proud of our efforts. Now you have several working walls that are barely updated and look scruffy. Nothing is mounted and most things are too small for us to read anyway. Everything hangs of the side of the display board. It's like you are trying to make them look raw and edgy – trying to prove excellent learning is taking place. It sucks.

I hope this helps.

Thank you,

Fake Pupil

As you can tell, this pupil is deluded so it is imperative we find out who wrote it. Obviously, completely ignore the advice they have given. The pressures you are all under are completely valid and keeps me in my job.

Fake Headteacher

Newsletter No.17 - Why Are You Leaving?

Dear Staff,

I am extremely sorry that I had to shut the school today. But don't worry, lesson observations and pupil progress meetings have been postponed until next week. I have emailed you some spreadsheets to complete as the snow shouldn't stop you from working at home.

I have heard rumours that many of you are not enjoying your job as much as you used to. In fact, many of you have expressed your desire to go part time or even leave teaching altogether. Some have already gone on supply. I don't understand.

Since arriving at the school, I have worked so hard to ensure consistency and to raise the standard of teaching and learning. I want to move up the academy ladder and I am doing it in record time too.

For example, I have instructed everyone they need to print off learning objective slips for every lesson. They must include a success criterion and some form of self-assessment (traffic lights) that the children can tick. After lessons, the slips must be highlighted green, orange or pink to prove the level of learning that took place in the lesson. I regularly look for these during book scrutinies.

I am trying to help you. I tell you exactly how to mark your books. You must use a black pen, use a range of coloured highlighters and two stars and a wish must be written daily. I even bought you all some lovely stampers in order to place a whole range of feedback on their work. I will check you are using them.

Work must be deep marked every three and a half lessons and it should always be initialled, so I know who taught the lesson. I have given you a long list of suggested feedback comments that I will check you are using. Next steps must be recorded daily using a hand drawn ladder or steps and children must always use a purple pen to prove they are editing. I am trying to help you improve your marking.

I tell you the schemes of work and textbooks you must use for reading, writing and maths. I have now introduced a spelling scheme that I expect everyone to use even if you don't like it. I tell you how long each unit of work should last and advise you on the best way to deliver it. I have made it clear how often work should be published and what colour pen they must use. Before a unit of work is taught, I ask you to carry out cold tasks and hot tasks after the unit is taught (but many weeks away from the point of teaching).

I insist every maths lesson must be mastery, concrete, pictorial and abstract. Children should demonstrate fluency and be able to work in random pairs all the time. I tell you what resources to use because they accompany the schemes of work. Children must be able to reason, and I expect to see bar models everywhere. One staff meeting was allocated last year for training on this, so I expect to see it competently embedded into your lessons. Can't you see how I am trying to help you?

I have shown you how to set targets for all the children, for all the core subjects and when to review these. This is in addition to the online assessments you carry out and the paper tests I make you administer. None of them really match up so I appreciate it's hard to get a true picture of their abilities as the data is inconsistent.

Online tracking assessment must be updated all the time to show progress. I will use this data for pupil progress meetings. I appreciate there's barely enough time to teach and embed all of the objectives for your year group, but I insist that children are only meeting expected standards if they do some work that is away from the point of teaching and you have seen evidence of it seven times. I am sure this is easily managed.

You must upload photos and videos to prove progress. They are stored on the online tracking program for no one to look at. Ofsted might spend hours looking through your photos and videos. I realise you only bring books for moderation meetings and we never sit in front of the online tracking program to look at your photos and videos. However, please upload all evidence. I am trying to help you improve.

I even tell you what your planning should look like and what to include. I tell you where to save it and how to annotate your plans to prove you are assessing daily. You must use the school's long-term, medium-term and short-term planning formats and I will ask to see them regularly. I am trying to help you.

I also tell you exactly what to put up on your displays. I have told you several times what needs to be seen on the display boards. I even have checklists that I use when I am on learning walks. You must follow my display policy.

You must have working walls for spelling, maths and writing. I need to see a growth mindset display and a learning journey display that is often more empty than full. I do not want to see static displays in your classroom. Displays must be regularly updated - daily if possible. Any text on display must be 50% handwritten and 50% typed but make sure it is the agreed school font. Work must be mounted following the school's policy and the agreed backing paper must be used. I am trying to help you.

Please see my latest policy on homework. I have decided what homework each year group is set, how often it is set and how it is marked. That reminds me, please write weekly letters to post on the website telling parents what you are teaching for a particular week. I am sure they all read them. I am trying to help you.

I even carry out learning walks, carry out regular book scrutinies, watch you teach, invite you to pupil progress meetings, give you feedback on how you teach, carry out year group mocksteds, where I pull apart everything that you are doing in that year group and make sweeping changes over night - making you feel terrible in the process.

But despite all this effort on my part, many of you still want to find other jobs. There is a teaching recruitment crisis. I don't understand. With so many leaders like myself, teaching has never been easier. I tell you how to do everything and hold you accountable if you don't do it. It will always be your fault even though you have no say in most things. Your pay will be affected if you don't adhere fully to my policies. I am trying to help you.

I am sure over time, things will settle down. But in the meantime, please just do exactly what I say, and we will get along just fine.

During the next few years, I would like to address staff well-being and workload but everyone seems fine at the moment so that can wait. Nobody has personally complained to me, so I assume you are all coping.

Don't forget to email your spreadsheets by lunchtime today. I have decided to do a learning walk tomorrow if the school is open so make sure you are ready for that. An academy director is visiting next week so I need to impress her.

So please stop all this talk of wanting to leave. I am trying to help you.

Thank you,

Fake Headteacher

Newsletter No.18 – Outstanding School

Dear Staff,

I haven't written a newsletter for some time as I have spent a long time away with academy duties. I trust the school has been operating effectively in my absence.

As you know, I really want my school to get at least a good grading from Ofsted. However, to impress the academy, I am pushing for an outstanding grade this year. These are some of the key words from my plan:

- Book scrutinies
- Green highlighters
- Pink highlighters
- Purple pens
- Deep dives
- Lesson observations
- Headteacher learning walks
- Deputy Head learning walks
- Governor learning walks
- Data drops
- Assessments
- Subject leader learning walks
- Pupil progress meetings
- Working walls
- Non-negotiables
- Performance related pay
- Mastery
- Data
- Testing
- Triangulation
- RAG rating
- Pupil premium
- Evidence

- Moderation meetings
- Photos
- Learning objective printed slips
- Peer assessment
- Timetables
- Talk partners
- Consistency
- Fronted adverbials
- Tracking
- Class blogs
- Pre-teach
- Newsletters
- Videos
- HMI visits
- DFE visits
- Mixed ability
- Ofsted
- Two stars and a wish
- Verbal feedback evidence
- VF stampers
- Annotations of conversations with pupils
- Responding to feedback
- Whole class reading
- Growth mindset
- SEN folders
- SEN records
- House points
- Interventions
- Whole class feedback
- Same day interventions
- Next steps
- Wider curriculum
- SPAG
- Cursive style
- Dojos
- Merits
- Behaviour log

- Behaviour flow chart
- Concrete
- Pictorial
- Abstract
- Talk before writing
- When to share the learning objective
- How to share the learning objective
- Workload
- Coaching
- Mentoring
- Lesson feedback
- Vocabulary
- Traffic lights
- Tool kits
- Inference
- Coding
- Questioning
- Times tables
- Spelling
- Success criteria
- TA deployment
- Restraining
- Break duty
- Class assemblies
- Reports
- Parents evening
- Discos
- Christmas fairs
- Summer fairs
- Film nights
- Concerts
- Productions
- Classroom displays
- Marking
- Homework
- Topic overviews
- Weekly overviews

- Teaching gymnastics
- Teaching RE
- Staff meetings
- Morning diary meetings
- Inspectors
- Timetables
- Updating files on the server
- Photocopying rules
- Homework
- Sports day
- Modal verbs
- Meetings
- Exceeding
- Phonics
- Modelling maths
- SATs
- STEM
- NRICH
- White Rose
- Numicon
- Reasoning
- Exit tickets
- Fluency
- Modelling writing
- Editing
- Redrafting
- Laptop trolleys
- Long date
- Short date
- Fractions
- Planning meetings
- Key stage meetings
- Parent workshops
- TA time
- Pay freeze
- UPS burden on budget
- Academies

- Accountability
- Requires improvement
- Staying good
- Staying outstanding
- Book fair
- Science day
- Art day
- Evidence for kite marks
- Action plans
- Development plans
- SEF
- Spreadsheets
- Progress
- Budgets
- Flip chart paper
- Cheap glue sticks
- Cheap white board pens
- Feedback stampers
- Away from the point of teaching
- Deep mark
- Passwords
- Usernames
- Reading diaries
- Homework books
- Book corners
- Before school club
- Breakfast club
- After school clubs
- Booster groups
- Common exception words
- Emails
- Middle leadership
- Weekend CPD events
- Quality texts
- Tick boxing
- Playing the game
- Targets

- School directors
- Attendance
- Test analysis
- Performance management
- Pay based on your data
- Micro-managing

I hope that all made sense. Sleep well.

Fake Headteacher

Newsletter No.19 - Independent Writing

Dear Staff,

I trust you are all relaxing and working hard at the same time. My bosses are very pleased with how I am running the school. They particularly liked how I took down children's work from my office wall and replaced it with data analysis charts and predictions. I have to say, it does look great. It'll look good when Ofsted walk in. It clearly shows I am all over it.

I haven't forgotten to discuss workload and staff well-being with you. I thought it best to do so when the four members of staff, who are off with stress, return and the two other teachers, who are on UPS3, leave.

In order to make your life easier, I have updated our independent writing policy. I have called it 'Ten Steps to Success'. I expect the writing to improve so make sure you read the advice very carefully. If the independent writing improves then I shall be very pleased, and you will avoid capabilities and a pay freeze. Do what you need to do.

Independent Writing Policy: Ten ideas for collecting evidence

1. A pupil chooses to write a story in golden time. She sits on her own, plans a story, writes it and continues to redraft it. She hands it to the teacher who immediately opens the online tracking program and assesses it.

2. The teacher tells the class to write something. She doesn't mind what they write about and gives them some paper and pens. 'Show me some great sentences - without any additional help, videos, photos or stories to inspire you.'

3. The teacher gives pupils a photograph of a haunted house to write about. Pupils share ideas before choosing what genre to pick for their writing. No word mats or spelling sheets are given.

4. Same as number 3 but pupils are given word mats with grammatical features and spellings on.

5. Pupils are given a video or a photograph to inspire some writing. They will all write a story. The teacher orally rehearses another story (everyday) so pupils can easily write their own based on the modelled text. The teacher then models how to plan the story. No word mats are allowed. The teacher gives verbal feedback throughout to help improve the story.

6. Same as number 5 but pupils are given word mats with grammatical features and sentence starters on.

7. Same as numbers 5-6 but written feedback also given.

8. Same as numbers 5-7 but the teacher writes extra advice on post it notes so there is no evidence of the extra support given.

9. Same as numbers 5-8 but pupils are told to redraft work several times with a purple pen to show self-editing based on verbal feedback and post it notes feedback (so there is no evidence of the support given).

10. Same as numbers 5-9 but pupils told exactly what words would be good to include in their story! The teacher adds extra purple pen edits at home to please the up-coming book scrutiny.

I hope this helps. Did I miss anything? Please let me know. If anyone asks in moderation meetings, pupils do No.1 in lessons. However, I encourage you to do No.10. Play the game people. Play the game.

I look forward to reading their independent writing.

Fake Headteacher

Newsletter No.20 - Updated Pay Policy

Dear Staff,

Thank you so much for working so hard during the first few weeks of term. I have heard a few of you raising your voices in the classroom this week, which can only mean the honeymoon period is over. I am sure you are already thinking about half-term and discussing what other jobs you could be doing instead with your family.

Stick with it though because I have some exciting news about your working conditions.

I have recently realised how much money each and every one of you are saving the school. In fact, you have contributed to tens of thousands of pounds being saved over the year (if not hundreds of thousands).

Let me explain.

You are legally bound to work 1,265 directed hours every year. This equates to 32.5 hours a week (see your payslip). And because you work 50 hours a week, that's 17.5 hours a week you work for free. Over 39 school term weeks, you work 682.5 hours for free. And when you divide the 682.5 hours you work for free over the year, this equates to 21 weeks you work for free.

Mind you, to be honest, you do get long holidays where you sit around doing very little. So actually, I should take away nine weeks' worth of hours from the 682.5 hours you work for free (I won't include the other 4 weeks as everyone else gets paid this as holiday - 13 weeks' school holiday in total).

So, nine weeks' worth of holiday hours equates to 292.5 hours over the year (9 weeks x 32.5 hours).

That's a lot of salary for not doing much eh. I will subtract these hours from the 682.5 hours you work for free each year. This still equates to a whopping 390 hours you *still* work for free.

So, 390 hours equates to 12 weeks working for me for free (390 divided by 32.5-hour week). That's 3 months of your own time that you somehow squeeze into the school year - for free. Your family must be so proud of you.

However, a special mention must go to the teachers who are working 55 hours a week. You are working a massive 22.5 hours a week for free. Using the above formula, that equates to 585 free hours you work for me. This equates to 15 weeks you work for free. Thank you.

And for the teachers who work 60 hours a week. Well, what can I say? You have saved me so much money, I can't begin to explain. You are working a massive 27.5 hours a week extra for free! Using the same formula, that equates to 780 free hours you work for me. This equates to 24 weeks you work for free.

Wow. Thank you so much.

Book scrutinies, lesson observations, learning walks, staff meetings, coaching plans, mentoring plans, action plans, team meetings and pupil progress meetings will continue as normal this term. I just need to read through some resignation letters that have appeared on my desk first.

I am sure some bright spark will pick me up on my calculations, but I don't mind. I am certain you work so many hours for free anyway. Well done all of you. I don't know why teachers are looking for 9-5 jobs - it sounds very dull.

All the best,

Fake Headteacher

Newsletter No.21 - Exit Interviews

Dear Staff,

I hope you all had a lovely half-term break. Thank you to those who responded quickly to my messages over the week. I don't really have friends or close family members to see so I tend to work instead.

Sadly, three members of staff resigned during half-term. I can't find better teachers to replace them so I will be employing two supply teachers and an unqualified teacher who can't find work. Because four members of staff also resigned in the summer, we will be revisiting all my recent policies on how I want the school to operate in tomorrow's staff meeting.

Some of the outgoing staff demanded exit interviews with a third party - not with me. Apparently, they wanted to be able to explain why they were leaving in an open and safe manner without fear of any future come back. They said they had mentioned briefly in their resignation letters why they were leaving but were worried that the governors and Ofsted wouldn't read them.

They were right to think that. I have to ensure positivity permeates through the school and I can't afford to rock the boat. I am not very good at listening and picking up on low morale in school. I stick to what I know and aggressively roll out my non-negotiables (or what the academy tells me to do).

I have decided to decline staff the opportunity to attend exit interviews. Instead, I have reminded them not to discuss with staff why they are leaving. In paragraph 45.3 of their contracts, it makes it very clear that *'staff should refrain from sharing or disclosing matters that would have a negative effect on the morale of the other teachers.'*

I have even made some teachers sign contracts to promise they will never talk about the real reasons why they are leaving. I paid them to go quietly and quickly.

No-one knows why all my staff are fed up and resigning, apart from me. Imagine if the governors, Ofsted, parents and prospective candidates knew the real reasons why my staff were leaving.

So, feel free to leave, but it will be done stealthily and with no comeback on me. Brilliant.

Just a reminder that unannounced learning walks, display and book scrutinies are operating every day until the end of term.

Kind regards,

Fake Headteacher

Newsletter No.22 - I Am Sorry

Dear Staff,

When I arrived at your school five years ago, your SATs data was average. You told me that your curriculum was at the heart of the school. You told me the pupils needed a good, well balanced curriculum to cater for the many complex needs of the pupils.

You told me that you chose not to run excessive booster groups and after school SATs clubs. You told me that you only did mocks two weeks before SATs to minimise pupil stress. You told me that the staff were amazing and had an excellent relationship with the pupils and parents.

However, I ignored all that. I was asked to improve the SATs data and to prevent the school slipping into requires improvement.

So, I quickly introduced an excessive focus on grammar, writing, reading and maths. I chose to ignore your concerns about sacrificing foundation subjects in order to improve data each half-term.

I introduced excessive testing and tracking analysis software across the whole school. Many pupils who excelled in subjects such as music, art, DT, PE etc, were suddenly failing at school and as a result, behaviour at the school took a nosedive.

To prove my impact further, I introduced a long list of non-negotiables that were designed not to necessarily improve teaching and learning, but to impose authority and consistency. You became robots.

You told me that many new initiatives I introduced were not based on research but based on my own personal ideas.

Many of you started to get anxious and became disillusioned with how the school was being run. You could see the damage I was doing, and you were powerless to stop it. You knew I would put you on an action plan if you questioned my decisions.

The staff room became a toxic place where you regularly off-loaded.

Pupil progress meetings became the norm. I would mentally beat you about your data and made you feel inadequate about your teaching.

Some of you went off sick. Some of you resigned. Some of you cried. Some of you played the game. Some of you cheated in tests to keep me happy.

In a very short space of time, I turned the school upside down. Great teachers will never teach again, and others have lost their confidence.

Our SATs results went up slightly, but pupil numbers continued to fall as they left for other schools. I now have a distant relationship with the parents and the pupils don't really connect with me.

Now the curriculum has become the new thing and not so much to do with data. You told me all this when I started. I wish I had listened. To be honest, I didn't know any different.

But you were right. Your school was already doing fantastic things. Your priorities were spot on. Ironically, if Ofsted had visited your school back then, with the new framework they appear to be working from now, you may have got outstanding.

I am sorry to all the teachers who left teaching because of me.

I am sorry to all the teachers who had long periods of sick leave because of anxiety.

I am sorry that my naive policies were introduced.

They didn't work.

I am sorry.

Fake Headteacher

Newsletter No.23 - Trust Me

Dear Governors,

In light of our recent Ofsted grading, I would like to reassure you that I am determined to turn things around.

I have outlined my plans below:

- I will increase the number of planned learning walks.

- I will increase the number of unannounced learning walks.

- I will introduce coaching for all staff. I will visit lessons every week and tell staff how to improve.

- I will ensure staff type up, print and stick long, lengthy learning objective slips in all books.

- I will insist staff use green and pink highlighters to prove teacher feedback has occurred.

- I will insist pupils use purple pens three times a week to prove they have edited their work.

- I will dictate to staff what every display board must look like and how often they need to be updated.

- I will introduce another set of symbols and codes for staff to use when marking books - which must be seen in books every week.

- My 4-page book scrutiny checklist will be used to root out teachers who are underperforming and to keep more experienced teachers (who like to do their own thing) in line.

- Experienced staff will not be allowed to utilise any of their experience. They will teach how I say. They will mark how I say etc.

- Book scrutiny will occur fortnightly and staff will receive detailed written feedback on how they are doing. If time allows, I will look at pupil progress in books. But they will mostly focus on the non-negotiables set out in the book scrutiny checklist.

- All maths lessons will look identical across the school following the scheme of work I have recently invested in. Teachers will not deviate from the lesson structure I have introduced.

- All literacy lessons will look identical across the school following the scheme of work I have recently invested in. Teachers will not deviate from the lesson structure I have introduced.

- Actually, this applies to most subjects. Staff will teach how I say from now on.

- PPA time will now be used more productively with staff emailing me a report describing how they used their time. Staff must work in the PPA room where I can pop in to monitor their efforts.

- Staff meetings will now overrun by half an hour every week to enable us to investigate areas of weakness in more detail.

- Pupil progress meetings will be introduced and occur every six weeks. These will now happen at lunchtime to minimise disruption to lessons.

- Staff will be held completely accountable for ensuring accelerated progress for all pupils. Consequences such as capability measures and the freezing of pay rises will be introduced.

- At least 40% of staff will be on a support plan at any one time.

- All staff will be told to visit other schools to watch staff teach lessons. It ticks a box at least.

- We will re-write our curriculum every July.

- To save money, I will focus my attention on the UPS staff. It will be relatively straight forward to put pressure on them to leave. All adverts for new staff will attract naive NQTs. They will conform much more willingly. Well, for about two years at least.

I am confident my plan will quickly turn things around.

You must understand that the morale of staff will drop, and it will feel quite toxic for a while. However, it's one big game we must play to ensure Ofsted are happy.

Turnover of staff will increase but you must think long term.

Trust me. I will deliver.

Fake Headteacher

Newsletter No.24 - You Must Run a Club

Dear Staff,

I am very disappointed that many of you are refusing to run morning, lunchtime and after school clubs.

They are an important part of school life and pupils deserve the chance to enrich their school experience by attending them.

It also helps us compete with our rival schools. It makes us look bad if we don't offer the same level of extra-curricular sessions.

Parents expect it now.

I realise that many children who come to clubs don't really want to be there and don't fully engage in the activities you have planned. But it is what it is. Parents have a right to cheap childcare. You are not allowed to refuse to have particular children in your club.

I appreciate that you have already had a long day teaching and dealing with countless problems and challenges. But clubs are vital to our reputation.

If some parents are late every time picking up children, then that's just tough. What's an extra 15 minutes anyway?

You said I had increased your workload too much to justify not running a club. That's just ridiculous. Book scrutinies, learning walks and display checks are part of your job now. Get over it.

I understand that many of you are on support plans or have difficult targets to meet but surely you can give up a couple of hours a week to run clubs?

I hope you feel guilty.

UPS staff must run a club. I don't know whether I am allowed to say that but that's how it is. NQTs will be expected to run a club but not until three weeks in.

I would love to run a club but managing a school keeps me busy and I simply don't have time.

I expect all staff to have signed up to at least one club by Friday.

Fake Headteacher

Newsletter No.25 - Consistency

Dear Staff,

Thank you for your hard work this half-term. It's been a long one for sure. Hopefully the four extra twilight sessions on reducing workload has helped.

We did identify a few areas where you could reduce workload but remember, it mustn't affect whole school policies on our journey to become even better than better.

For example, remember to rearrange the tables into rows, groups or in a horseshoe shape depending on what subject you are teaching. I realise it's a faff but it's something I can say we do to improve teaching and learning.

Remember, you must follow the strict timings set out for each maths lesson: teacher input 15 mins, buddy work 10 mins, independent work 15 mins, mini plenary 5 mins, 10 mins buddy work, 5 mins plenary. It's a whole school approach, so stop watches will be used on learning walks to monitor.

Timings for literacy and other subjects are slightly different so ensure you check the current non-negotiables sheet in the staffroom.

We have recently introduced a scheme for guided reading and phonics and the format of lessons must be followed to the letter. I understand it might not suit how you want to teach but I am looking for a whole school approach. It's not perfect, but it's safer than letting you all plan your own thing.

Remember, displays must look identical. I realise it stops you being creative and, but I really do need consistency across the school. I need to be 100% sure that when I show someone around, I can confidently say how the classroom environment is impacting on the learning. If you are all doing your own displays, it's harder to talk about.

Remember, all books must look the same. We have talked at length about what I expect to see in all books. The six-page checklist has been up in the staffroom for many weeks now. Make sure you are following it.

Again, it's so much easier for me to talk about my impact on the school if all books look the same. If teachers are giving feedback in different ways, I won't be able to explain this confidently to visitors. It will make me look bad.

Consistency is the key. It may feel dull and rather boring teaching like this, but it's the future. Follow the rules.

You may feel the spark and magic of teaching has been sucked out of you. You're right. It is what it is at the moment.

Once we complete our journey to even better than better, I may be able to ease off. But I doubt it.

If you are still unsure, the 257-page rule book on how to teach at my school can be downloaded as a PDF on the server. Or, you can ask my PA for a hard copy.

Mocksted is planned for the first week back after half-term.

Have a lovely break. Try not to work too hard!

Fake Headteacher

Newsletter No.26 - Toxic Schools

Dear Staff,

Thank you so much for all of your hard work and the sacrifices you've made this term. Sadly, we say goodbye to another group of teachers. I am not allowed to discuss with you why they are leaving as they have signed whistle blowing contracts. However, I wish them well.

With so much attention on social media about 'toxic schools' I thought I might address this with you all to ease your mind. Some of you may not have worked in a toxic school before and want to know more. Some of you may have already experienced it and just want some more information. Some of you may feel our school is toxic. You're entitled to your opinion I suppose.

Stage 1: Confidence

It's important to remember that teachers who have experienced working in toxic schools were once very confident. They had successful teaching placements and probably worked in other schools where they were valued. This is why they find it hard to adjust when faced with the issues toxic schools present. Nearly all teachers who struggle adapting in toxic schools were once very confident in the classroom. Remember that.

Stage 2: Shock

This is arguably the hardest part of the process. Suddenly, you are given lists of non-negotiables and subjected to increased lesson observations (disguised as learning walks). Book scrutiny and display board checks are carried out all the time and pupil progress interrogations become more frequent.

Teachers' pay is often frozen and UPS staff start to feel the heat because the school can't afford to keep them. Support plans are dished out frequently and the toxicity begins to creep in. Teachers begin to moan to family and friends and the spiral of negativity accelerates. Good teachers are told they are not good anymore. Nothing is good enough.

Stage 3: Defiance

Some teachers will resist the changes for a while. They will speak up in staff meetings and start up secret social media chat rooms in order to let off steam. One brave teacher will speak up a little too much and experience the wrath of the management team.

Once staff realise the consequences for wanting to debate issues affecting well-being and workload are severe, they think twice. Defiance doesn't last long. Teachers panic and mentally hide, and then move onto Stage 4.

Stage 4: Tolerance

This is where the real damage is done I'm afraid. The workload and accountability pressures by this point are in full swing and teachers know they can't fight back. Most are too worried to contact their unions and those who do, don't have the confidence the union will help them, so they give up. Staff now accept the school has changed and make a conscious decision (for the own sanity, professionalism and their personal relationships outside of school) to knuckle down and make the best of a crap situation.

The problem with this, is that it eats away at your job satisfaction. Your confidence begins to wane, and you start resenting your job. You might even start to hate your job. It's clear that some staff members are being targeted. Who will be next? But you keep going because you that's what you are good at. You haven't failed at anything before. Teachers naturally want to do well. It's part of their work ethic.

Stage 5: Exhaustion

Sadly, after months of tolerating the new regime and trying to tick all the boxes that have been thrust at staff, teachers begin to feel exhausted. Not just 'teacher tired'. I mean, absolutely mentally and physically exhausted. The problem is, they've given up seeing friends, they've stopped going to the gym, they're drinking more, they're staying up late trying to keep up with the demands of the job, and relationships at home start to wobble.

They can't think straight anymore. They have lost their mojo and find it hard to know what the best course of action is to take. The only thing they do know, is they must keep up at school otherwise they will be given another support plan and they don't need that. Once everything starts to affect their sleep, Stage 6 kicks in.

Stage 6: Stress

Your partner starts to worry about you. Your friends *would* say something, but you haven't seen them for months. After weeks of not sleeping properly, teachers find themselves on the brink of a breakdown – only they don't know what this feels like, so they don't recognise it for what it is. They will eventually, but by then, it's too late.

If nothing changes at school soon, teachers slowly become more and more stressed, to a point where they might suddenly break down without warning. They will feel confused and scared. This has never happened to them before. They will start to cry and won't understand why they can't get to work.

 They will still tell people they are fine because they don't really know what to say. Some teachers will seek advice immediately form the doctor and will inevitably burst into tears in front of them. The doctor will sign them off for two weeks.

In some cases, this is enough for a teacher to realise that they need to leave their school and do so the following term. Others however, will struggle. The damage has been done and it's hard to come back from that. They may have longer periods off with depression and anxiety. They may never come back to teaching or go on supply for a while. Others stay for a few more years. They just about cope but they are extremely miserable.

Stage 7: Guilt

Stage 6 is tough. Really tough. There are so many decisions teachers must make. Not just for themselves but for their family too. One of the immediate emotions experienced by teachers, after going through this whole process, is guilt and sadness. You feel bad because you have (wrongly) labelled yourself as a failure. You can't cope with the job you always wanted to do. You've let the pupils down. You've let your colleagues down. Your finances are taking a hit.

Teachers start to feel bad about everything. They forget it wasn't their fault. It's really not – remember Stage 1? Your emotions overpower you. Teachers find it hard to think about anything else now. It has consumed them. It's emotionally draining. You can't see a positive future. Not yet anyway.

Stage 8: Relief

Stage 8 is a strange one. How could you possibly feel relieved after everything you've been through? But it's true. As horrid an experience as it was, teachers soon begin to realise how toxic the school was. They start to feel relieved they don't work there anymore. They start to worry for staff still there and keep in touch with them all the time. They start to advise other teachers to get out before they are forced out. You start to get a little perspective on the whole matter.

You begin to realise that you were bullied, or forced out, or your anxiety was a serious issue that you had to come to terms with (and that's ok). You start to feel better. Honestly, you do. You feel relieved. But...

Stage 9: Anger

This is really tough because teachers find it hard to let this one go - for very good reasons. You feel relieved you've left. You feel awakened by your new sense of well-being and can see a better future ahead. A future less stressed and one of hope. But you start to feel angry. Teachers will feel very bitter about the process they experienced. They may seem fine and will say how pleased they are to 'get out'. But they will be pissed off.

What happened to them was a direct result of someone's misguided non-negotiables policy, added with a hunger and drive to raise standards in a heavy handed and insensitive manner. They will feel cheated out of a career that they cared so much about. Only now do they wish they had fought back at the time.

They play out the scenarios in their head and plan the things they should have said. What's worse, is they probably could have kicked SLT's arse, but you don't know that at the time.

When you feel vulnerable, you do what you can to survive. Teachers would love to go back in time and react very differently, but the moment has passed. Over time they will feel less angry about it. Actually, no they won't. That's rubbish. It stays with them for a long, long time.

Stage 10: Prioritising

Despite all this, teachers will come out of it with a new set of values. They will demand they see their friends more often, they will give their partner more attention and will spend more time with their children. They soon realise that money isn't everything and will say things like 'My money is bad but I'm happier.' They will inspire other teachers to rethink their lifestyles. If you reach Stage 10, you will be more at one with yourself and understand what's important to you. Life is too short.

Finally:

I hope you found this information useful. I look forward to seeing you all after Christmas. We will be focusing on accelerated progress, marking codes, deep marks and 3D working walls.

Fake Headteacher

Ofsted Inspector Chat No.1 – Books

Two inspectors are carrying out a book scrutiny during assembly.

These books look immaculate.

> Yes, I agree. Works of art.

I feel like I should be wearing gloves to protect them.

> Ha, ha. I know what you mean.

Just look at them. Printed learning objective slips with a success criterion, which pupils have traffic lighted to show us how they felt about their leaning. The teacher has written whether the work was done independently, with adult support or peer supported.

> I know. Every other page has been deep marked with pupils editing with purple pens and teacher comments indicating next steps with top tips to make accelerated progress.

Very impressive, I agree. Look here. The teacher has written VF to show when verbal feedback was given. It's everywhere.

> I saw that too. They've even written next to the letters VF, exactly what they said to the pupil and drawn an arrow to show us exactly what the pupil did in response. Brilliant.

There aren't any pages missing and every date is perfectly written and underlined with a ruler.

> The teacher has even made it very clear what the pupil did well by repeating the learning objective. *'You managed to use adverbs today like the LO said you were going to do.'*

That's dedication for you. Makes it so easy for us to make a judgement on the books and the impact the teacher is having.

I agree. I have just noticed that staff are required to initial every piece of work too to show they taught the lesson.

I love all these symbols they use too: little ladders for next steps, stars and magic wands for 2 stars and a wish, hearts for good sentences, emoji-like faces to show how the teacher feels about their work etc. Truly beautiful.

I especially love the use of highlighters. Over most of the work, the teacher has highlighted good bits in one colour and bits to improve in another. It makes it so obvious that the teacher is pushing the pupils on. It smacks us right in the face. Very clever.

It must take teachers hours every week to make these books look Ofsted ready.

Yes, you're right. They are very good.

Shame really though, don't you think - if we're really honest. I mean, would the pupil still make progress without any of these things?

Oh, I would have thought so. Teachers are very smart. They know their pupils really well and adjust lessons accordingly on a daily basis to ensure progress is made.

Yes, I agree. I know they give so much feedback in class to pupils.

So, it makes you wonder why they do all this work then. I mean, it would cut down on workload if they didn't need to do so much in books.

Yes. You might be on to something. Maybe we should say something?

What do you mean?

Well, if we can see that the books look overly worked on by teachers, because of an obsessive SLT who dictate how books should look in order to impress Ofsted, maybe we should pick up on this because of the impact it has on workload.

Wow. That would be interesting. Do you think it would work?

I think so. It's progress that we should be looking at over time. No one should worry about the other stuff. SLT should be doing the same. They must have a long list of non-negotiables for staff to follow to make the books look like this. It's crazy.

Can you imagine SLT being criticised in our report for creating excessive workload for teachers, just to make books look Ofsted ready.

Right. I think we've decided then.

Yup. That was really useful. Thanks for the chat.

I will call the boss right away and put forward our suggestions.

Brilliant. Cuppa?

Please. Any chocolate biscuits going?

Ofsted Inspector Chat No.2 – Book Scrutiny

Two inspectors are chatting about their imminent book scrutiny.

I've asked the head if we can use the empty classroom to carry out the book scrutiny.

Well done, we're going to need the space for sure.

I know. There's going to be hundreds of books piled up in there after break.

Did you ask staff for current books only?

I tried, but the head demanded we take in every single book so we can see progress over time.

Oh. That's not good. It's going to take us hours. We've only allocated 30 minutes.

I know. I might tell the head to ask staff to group the books for each pupil, so we don't have to spend ages finding the same pupils' books.

Staff won't like that. They already look stressed.

Have you read the school's detailed marking policy yet?

No. Anyway, I haven't got time to read it and then make sure every member of staff is implementing it.

I know. My friend is a head and constantly tells staff they must follow the marking policy to the letter because Ofsted will check.

I don't really care what the marking policy is to be honest. I haven't got time to check it's being implemented. That's not my job.

I agree - as long as progress is there.

Yeah. Absolutely.

I do hope they group pupils' books.

Me too. The school has 300 on roll.

We're going to need a bigger room.

The work that goes into making every single book Ofsted ready always baffles me.

I think we've only got time to look at a handful. That's some serious workload issues for staff eh.

Yup.

Right. We better get ready. I can see the first trolley of books arriving.

Good luck.

You too.

Teacher Letter No.1 - Book Scrutiny

Dear Fake Headteacher,

Thank you for emailing your newsletters on a Saturday morning. It's usually when we are relaxing with our families, so we don't always read them straight away. They have been thought provoking to say the least.

You are clearly an ambitious and passionate person who wants the prestige of being the Head of a good or outstanding school whatever the cost.

The thought of being a Head of a 'Requires Improvement' school can't be an easy one for you. Many of us have worked in these schools and it's not great.

I appreciate how hard your job must be, but my colleagues have asked me to respond to your newsletters as many of us have grievances with your policies.

You don't set aside time for us to discuss strategies to reduce workload or allow time to discuss how we could make our jobs less stressful, so I hope you don't mind giving up your Saturday morning to read my letter instead.

Initially, I was asked to write a general response to your newsletters, but many teachers had particular problems with your book scrutiny policy. Let me remind you of some of the things you expect to see in all our books. This is just the first page.

Could teachers make sure they have included:

- Short date
- Typed up learning objective slips for all subjects which are stuck in books every lesson
- Success criterion present

- Tool kits present
- Children responding in purple pen
- Green and pink highlighting
- Deep marking twice a week
- Peer assessment
- Child feedback
- Staff to initial all work
- Evidence of verbal feedback given
- Regular written next steps
- 2 stars and a wish present
- All spellings picked up on
- Marking code followed
- Every piece marked daily
- One piece of praise each week
- More able being stretched
- Barriers to learning being addressed
- Progress in grammar evident
- Photographic evidence whenever possible
- Evidence of children's understanding is checked, and intervention taken as a result
- Evidence of target setting
- Proof of teacher impact evident
- Evidence of pupil premium children being supported etc.

A Year 6 colleague was very upset this week because she was put on a coaching program. Her books did not meet your high standards during your latest book scrutiny, even though her class had made accelerated progress this half-term.

The standard of work her class produce is always exceptional. She responds to the needs of her children daily and adjusts her lessons accordingly. Her assessment for learning is outstanding and always has the children eating out of the palm of her hand. She regularly praises the children for their efforts and as a result, the behaviour of her class has dramatically improved.

Despite this, you have destroyed her confidence by criticising her methodology because her books didn't show enough green and pink highlighting and learning objectives weren't consistently typed up (the children had written them instead). Apparently, you told her she had forgotten to write the date on some pieces of work and some work had just been 'ticked'. You told her this was unacceptable.

Surely, the most important part of the job is that children make progress. If progress is clearly seen in pupils' books, especially accelerated progress, you must assume the teacher has done an exceptional job.

Progress like this doesn't just happen. You must assume they have intervened at the right times, pushed on the more able, applied a bit tough love when necessary, used appropriate humour and praise to motivate etc.

To criticise the teacher just because they didn't completely follow your book scrutiny guidance is ridiculous.

What does progress even mean? It can often look invisible, but it's happened. The fact that a child who needed constant reassurance and support in September now works completely independently with enthusiasm is progress. Their books won't show it but it's huge progress.

It is comparable to asking Lionel Messi to play in goal and then when he plays poorly, you make him a substitute and put him on a personal training program so he can improve his game.

He is punished because he cannot work in the way you have dictated. It is not natural for him to play in that position. He performs far better when he has the freedom to play in his favourite position. Dictating to teachers how to mark and give feedback to children is ludicrous.

If you looked at a teacher's set of books and no progress was evident over time, then you would be obliged to support that teacher by offering guidance on how to improve using strategies you saw fit.

Everyone understands this. You would need to intervene. However, most of us will show you good or better progress regardless of your marking policy.

You are currently asking all members of staff to play in the wrong position. Let them play in the position they prefer so they can show maximum effectiveness. Then judge them. Only then, are teachers fully accountable. Teachers are not marking books naturally.

Often, some teachers will skim through the books they are about to hand in for scrutiny and look for opportunities to write extra comments and add additional marking codes to make their books look better. I have. This is madness.

As you wander around the school at lunchtime, you will see teachers marking their books. Teachers are so worried now about their books, they are over-marking just in case they get too many 'reds' on their book scrutiny feedback.

It doesn't help when you repeatedly make comments like, 'You are not spending all lunchtime marking are you? Make sure you find time to eat and relax.'

When you have to mark literacy and maths every day (not to mention other books), and plan and prepare the next day's lesson, you can begin to see why lunchtime has become a good time to get work done. It is never a good time to work at lunchtime, but teachers have to.

When you throw in the pressure to run an after-school club and the pressure to attend additional meetings, it won't be long before teachers don't even make it to the staff room.

Most teachers I speak to are working at least 2 hours every night at home and most of Sunday evening. This is not healthy or desirable. Many teachers report they work 50-60 hours each week.

'It's all about the books,' is all we hear at the moment. But Ofsted have said they don't care what the books look like as long as teachers are following the school policy. As long as Ofsted see progress, that's all that counts. So why don't you change the book scrutiny checklist to something like:

- Progress will be the first thing I look for in your books - regardless of how you mark or the type of feedback that is evident.
- I trust you to support the children as necessary.
- I trust you will adjust lessons accordingly to meet all children's needs.
- I don't expect to see particular feedback comments in books as I know you spend most of your time telling your class how they have done and what they need to do to improve. You don't need to prove this.
- I don't need to see photographic evidence of when you went outside for a lesson or had the weighing scales out!
- I understand that some lessons will not be evidenced in books because you didn't do it in their books!
- I will expect to see progress in books.
- I will only intervene if progress is poor. Then you will mark how I tell you.
- I repeat, progress will be first thing I look for in your books - regardless of how you mark or the type of feedback that is given.
- If progress is present, you must be a caring and hardworking teacher who gets the best out of the children. Well done.

When Ofsted see progress in books, they will be very happy. They will be happy because teachers will have been following your (new one above) book policy.

And you wonder why staff are not attending as many school discos, fairs, film nights, clubs etc. They are exhausted and run down.

To tell a teacher they are ineffective because they have not managed to get enough 'greens' on your long book scrutiny checklist is outrageous.

Has a class made good progress? Yes?

Then perhaps you could tap into how that teacher achieved that progress and share this with the rest of us, instead of being such a control freak by demanding everyone must toe-the-line with your checklists in the name of consistency.

If your book scrutiny checklist ceased to exist, you would presumably expect to see very little progress in books? What a naive attitude to have. You are panicking. In some or most cases, you would probably see better progress because teachers would be free to spend more time on planning and resourcing their lessons more effectively.

In fact, your book scrutiny could look like:

Is good progress present over time?

- Yes
- No

It's that simple.

Thank you. I will of course be expecting an early morning meeting with you on Monday... gulp.

Fake Teacher

Teacher Letter No.2 - Moving Schools

Dear Fake Headteacher,

Another round of lesson observations and members of staff who have been at your school for several years, have perfected their lessons for you. They have endured many lesson feedback meetings with you and know exactly how to please you.

However, *your* philosophy isn't exclusive to good teaching. It's not the only way. Just because a teacher doesn't teach how you expect, it doesn't mean they are inadequate teachers. I have published this for new teachers at your school!

My advice to any colleague who is starting a new school is this:

See the Head on day one. Ask them to tell you what *they* want to see in your lessons. Find out if they like plenaries, whole class inputs, use of lolly sticks for questioning, mixed ability groups etc. Ask them what particular things they like to see in your lessons. What are they fans of? What don't they like?

Also, speak to the teachers who have been there a while. Ask them the same questions. It doesn't matter if you disagree with the Head's ideas. Learn them. Master them. Get good lesson feedback and stay under the radar. Then do what you do naturally day to day. Surely it doesn't matter how you teach? Yes. It does matter apparently.

My experience in my last four schools has been very different:

School 1:

- The Head wanted to see whole class inputs for ten minutes and a plenary for ten minutes - every lesson.

- The children had to be in ability groups and moved once every half-term if needed.
- You were expected to 'butterfly' teach and not to sit with a group.
- The learning objective had to be shared in the first minute.
- Children had to use whiteboards on the carpet to brainstorm ideas.
- Mark how you wanted to - you were trusted – use praise a lot.

If you did these things it would almost guarantee a good / outstanding lesson. I did. Yeah!

School 2:

I had cracked what a good lesson was! Well, that's what I thought! I failed my first observation based on what I had been told in my first school. I was devastated. It turned out, the Head at this school preferred:

- No learning objectives shared at the start as it told them too much straight away.
- No plenaries. Instead, several mini plenaries throughout the lesson.
- Sit with one group and concentrate on pushing their learning forward. Absolutely no 'butterfly teaching'.
- Group them by ability and provide evidence that children move groups throughout the week.
- Children to sit on chairs at all times - no carpet time as children get too distracted.
- Mark how you want as long as you use the school marking code.

It took me a while to re-program my style of teaching, but I mastered it and eventually I was consistently getting good observations.

School 3:

I arrived as a 'good' teacher and knew how to teach to a high standard. I was looking forward to my lesson observations because I knew what to do to impress the Head. *I failed my first two lesson observations!* It turned out, my new Head had very different ideas to my previous two Heads.

- No whole class input because it doesn't cater to all needs.
- No introduction - straight into group teaching.
- Teacher to stay with one ability group for the first 15 minutes, TA to another group and one group working independently.
- Three different learning objectives for each lesson for each ability group.
- No plenaries at all.
- No time to praise - just write targets.
- Children to stay in seats at all times so observer can track progress of each group (no drama, moving around to different activities etc).
- After you teach a group, move to the independent group and TA support class.
- Use coloured cups so you can see who needs help (green, orange, red).
- Follow the 5-page book scrutiny checklist in order to mark correctly and for books to look uniform across the whole school.

Bloody hell. I hated it. This made no sense to me at all. I argued that most of what they wanted to see was not for the children. I was put on a coaching program for 2 weeks where I watched an average teacher deliver the 'perfect' lesson. When I still couldn't quite master this new style during my next observation, I was threatened with capabilities. I left at Easter, very stressed and very confused. Still, I found a new job!

School 4:

By now, I had lost my identity as a teacher along with any confidence I once had. Who knows what I should be doing anymore? I decided to try and implement school 3's methods because it was obviously the new 'fad' and the academy knew their stuff, right? Wrong! I again failed my first lesson. The Head was very disappointed that a teacher with my experience taught the way I did.

- Why didn't you deliver a whole class input with their talk buddies (talk buddies?).
- Why were the children sitting in ability groups? Always mix them up.
- Never give children the same work - put a range of questions on the table for them to choose - avoids copying.
- Why didn't you use named lolly sticks to ask children questions? Some children put their hands up! We have a no hands up policy.
- You must use the visualiser every lesson and share the objective with the SEN before the lesson starts.
- Why haven't you praised the children in books?
- You must use your working wall during your lesson.
- I was surprised that the children had written their own learning objective in Year 5 - please type them up along with a success criterion that is longer than the writing the children will do for the lesson.
- Please refer to the 3-page book scrutiny checklist.

I was beginning to see a pattern! It didn't matter what I thought anymore. I just had to impress the observer. With so much pressure on Heads, I am now micro-managed. Most of what I do now is to please someone else. Most of how I teach has no direct correlation to my own teaching philosophy and this is why I am writing to you. It doesn't matter how I want to feedback or mark. I must do what I am told.

Since I have begrudgingly accepted this is how it is in a lot of schools (to do what they want to see), I regularly receive good feedback after observations. They include many techniques and fads I wouldn't naturally enforce, and my books are mostly 'good' (meaning I follow a ridiculous marking policy that is mostly for an observer and not for the children).

As sad as it is, my advice to anyone moving schools is to speak to your Head.

'Tell me exactly what you want to see in my lessons, and I will do it.'

'Tell me exactly how you want me to mark books and I will do it.'

Perhaps Fake Headteacher, you could make this very clear to all new teachers? Be honest and tell them what you want to see straight away. It's a whole lot easier and doesn't affect teachers' confidence or want to make them leave teaching.

Kind regards,

Fake Teacher

Teacher Letter No.3 - Then and Now

Dear Fake Headteacher,

Many of us have been discussing why we are not enjoying teaching quite as much as we used to.

We used to mark with the nearest pen we could find.

Suddenly, we all had to use the same colour pen. Then, we were all bought the same pen, so the books all looked the same. Now we use green and pink highlighters to show the children what they did well and what they need to do to improve. It's a great way to prove your impact apparently.

We used to tick good words or sentences as we read work and if necessary, added a comment. A simple marking code was used.

The children used to use pencil or pen and edit with the same pencil or pen.

Now, children write in pen or pencil and if they want to improve their work, they must find a purple polishing pen. The children ask us, 'Why are we using purple pens?' We tell them it is a good way to prove the teacher is having an impact on the work and shows very clearly to Ofsted the children have had opportunities to re-draft.

We used to know how the lesson went and who needed support the next day. We would see the gaps and plan appropriately.

Now, we have to write next steps and targets every five minutes and allow children to respond to that advice. Some schools have dedicated time in the day for children to respond to the written feedback given (outside of normal lesson time).

I was put on a coaching program recently because the Head said my class had made excellent progress. I was confused. He said although the children had made excellent progress, I hadn't made it clear in their books the impact I was having! Not enough two stars and a wish apparently. I needed to make it clear what verbal feedback I was giving and to make more use of think pink and great green to highlight the impact I was having.

We used to write 'Well done' or 'Excellent work today,' and knew exactly what pupils had to learn the next day to improve. We didn't need to constantly tell them what they hadn't done.

'Well done' is frowned upon is some schools now. We now have to write next steps or prove we know how to move their learning forward by writing targets and advice in their books. We feel guilty only writing congratulatory comments.

Of course, we marked pieces that needed marking but only when they needed marking. Now, we are told we must 'deep mark' once a week. No one really knows what this even looks like. It has become part of our book scrutiny checklist.

The children in Key Stage 2 would always write a title.

That would be it. A title. Three words maximum. It would take thirty seconds to do and it was a good opportunity to remind them how to write titles, how to use correct capital letters and how to use a ruler to underline. Of course, the title didn't tell the whole picture but then the title didn't need to prove to an observer what the children were learning about. In most cases, it was bloody obvious.

We shared the learning objective in the lesson and always discussed what was needed for the writing to be successful (success criteria).

Now we have success criteria and toolkits that must be placed in books. I don't think they need to be in books. I think they just reassure you and Ofsted that we have good subject knowledge. It is something you look for during book scrutiny.

Now, you insist we type up lengthy learning objective slips. But I think it tells children too much straight away. There is no discovery. They are not for the children. They are to make the books look nice and prove to Ofsted how good our lessons are. It just adds to our workload.

Some schools ask the children to write the learning objective. But, they are still too long, and some argue that it is a waste of valuable learning time.

We miss very short titles! Common sense please.

Our planning would have a learning objective on with a few bullet points as to how the lesson might go.

Now, we have to write out a success criterion, write down the questions we will ask the children, make it clear who our SEN and Pupil Premium children are, write down what resources we need, how we will support the more able, give instructions for our teaching assistants, write down what group our teaching assistants will teach and other such nonsense. It's like being a student again.

To make it worse, we never look at this plan during the week. It gets saved on the server and re-written the following year. We have suggested several times that we should only plan the first lesson in detail as we have no idea how the week will pan out. And after that, we *write* out the rest of the week as we go. But you still insist that we type up weekly plans, 'What if you are sick one day?' Grrr.

We used to enjoy discussing work with the children.

Now you expect us to record everything the children say. You even have comment slips that we must carry around with us in case a child says something interesting. It's because we need to collect evidence for everything as we can't be trusted.

For example, my children tried to count in multiples of 100. I ticked off who could do it. Excited, because so many could already do it, you told me to individually film them and upload it to our data program as good evidence. I am the evidence. They could do it!

I told you about Child A last week who clearly explained why the author had used particular words to express an emotion. You told me to write down everything he said as proof. Now, when I am teaching reading, I spend more time writing down what pupils are saying rather than actively listening to them. We used to have a tick list to say if pupils could discuss authors' use of language. I would put a tick next to Child A's name. Easy. I am the evidence. They did it!

After children had edited the work we had marked, children would publish it. The work would then be put up on the wall to motivate children and boost their self-esteem.

Now you are lucky if you see any published work on the wall as we must prove our impact by continually updating working walls - raw displays that prove how much learning is taking place. If Ofsted come in, it will be clear how focused we are and prove we have good subject knowledge. Children don't really look at them and it's a pain in the rear trying to keep them up to date.

If you are lucky, you might have completed working walls for a few days before they are stripped naked again ready for the following unit of work. Give us exciting static displays and children's work on the wall any day.

We would have lovely conversations with our classes about how they felt about their learning.

We would know who was struggling in class and support as necessary. Children would tell us when they got stuck. Now you want me to find time every lesson for children to write a sentence about how they felt about their learning to prove they have 'pupil voice.'

They write Ofsted friendly comments like 'perfect level for me' or 'this was a good challenge' etc. They are not allowed to write 'this work was fun' or 'easy' (meaning they enjoyed it).

We now must have red, orange and green coloured pencils on the tables for children to draw faces about how they felt about their learning. We already know of course, but I must allow time for this in the lesson.

Often, they choose the wrong colour for many complicated reasons to do with self-esteem or over confidence. In some schools, the children place their book in a tray which are labelled 'I get this, I need help or More challenge please.' But we already know how they got on because we are good at our jobs.

We used to know who needed to be pushed or supported the next lesson.

Now you want us to use exit passes.

Children have participated in the lesson and produced work in their books. As they leave, you want them to answer another written question as a way of assessing their learning. But I already know. You insist that exit passes are brilliant for practical work so you can also assess their learning. But you also insist that children need to learn in a 'concrete' (practical) manner first before moving onto 'pictorial' work before finally moving on to 'abstract' work. So, by giving them an 'abstract' question after a practical concrete lesson is flawed.

It seems like another fad. But it is now part of your book scrutiny checklist, so we better do it. Workload.

It was always assumed if you were the teacher of a class, you had taught the lesson.

Now, you insist we must initial every piece of work the pupil completes. So that's 30 pupils x 4 lessons a day on average. That's 120 times we have to initial work. Imagine receiving 120 books on your desk to initial every day? How about only supply teachers initial the work? Easy.

We were allowed to put up displays we chose.

Now we have a list of displays you expect to see in every classroom. It's very boring. We pay lip service to it but because we don't have real ownership. We don't put as much effort into them anymore.

We used to be trusted.

Now we are micro-managed with non-negotiables, book scrutiny checklists and learning walks.

Kind regards,

Fake Teacher

Teacher Letter No.4 - Data Obsessed

Dear Fake Headteacher,

Our school was a happy school. The staff were brilliant. The previous Head was inspiring. I loved teaching there.

The curriculum was at the heart of the school. The curriculum was fabulous and pupils, who had a lot of emotional and social challenges, loved the school.

The Head didn't agree with SATs, so she didn't invite children to attend after school booster groups or spend most of Year 6 revising and preparing the pupils to pass a test. Call it naivety? Call it strong leadership?

After several years of low SATs scores, an academy took over and everything changed.

Within 6 months, the Head resigned. Within 8 months, the deputy resigned. Within 18 months, 10 members of staff resigned, either through ill health or found other jobs. Including me.

Then *you* were appointed (after 3 interim academy Heads in the space of 3 months - they all mysteriously disappeared - the academy way?).

The problem was you assumed the teaching and learning was terrible because of the low SATs scores. However, the issue was a philosophy. A philosophy that concentrated on the curriculum and not tests. A few tweaks here and there, to satisfy the need to improve good SATs scores, would have been enough to play the game. But you didn't. If only you had taken the time to find out.

Instead, you told us:

- to scrap most of our foundation subject teaching
- to ensure we had 4 ability groups for every lesson
- not to deliver whole class inputs - target groups only
- to write A4 plans the night before (with written annotations as proof of AfL)
- to photocopy these plans and hand them in on a Friday
- to hand in a timetable every week so you knew what we were teaching
- to have 4 different learning objectives for every lesson
- to use random named lolly sticks to ask pupils questions
- that teaching assistants must not sit with one group for more than 10 minutes
- that written praise was banned in books (focus more on next steps)
- that all work must be signed by the teacher and the learning objective must be highlighted green or orange to show whether the pupil understood the work
- that the use of green and pink highlighters must be used every day for marking
- that pupils must use purple pens 3 times a week in response to teacher feedback
- to attend a morning meeting at 8:30am twice a week to 'touch base' with each other
- to attend pupil progress meetings every 6 weeks
- to print off learning objectives slips that were often longer than what the pupils wrote in the lesson (description of the task, self-evaluation, success criteria etc.)
- to write verbal feedback in books whenever we gave advice to a pupil and then to write down exactly what we said - and what they said back!
- that Ofsted would crucify us if we didn't do all the things you told us to do because 'that's what they're looking for'
- our power points had to have the school logo on and use the agreed font style

- that you would do unannounced learning walks every week and use a 15-point checklist we had to be seen to be doing every time
- we would be put on an action plan if we didn't fulfil the 15-point checklist
- that had to prove any practical lesson we taught by taking photos - and stick them in books with annotations
- to tell parents that their child was below standard for their age before the end of September and invite the child to attend after school booster groups every Wednesday and Friday (run by staff)
- there would be book scrutinies every 6 weeks with written feedback on what was wrong (mostly!)
- that lunchtime was being shortened from 1 hour to 45 minutes to give more time for learning
- we had to write small ladder shapes and two stars and a wish in their books at least 3 times a week to make it clear to Ofsted the teachers knew how to move the learning forward
- we had to travel 2 hours to another school in the academy to observe other teachers
- we had to improve the behaviour of the pupils (that had unsurprisingly worsened since your arrival) using a complicated A3 flowchart of what actions to follow and when to follow them. It was so complicated, no-one bothered.
- we had to write reports on pupils who were misbehaving - to build up evidence for future exclusions (5 exclusions were made in your first 12 months)
- we weren't allowed to display pupils' work because it didn't help children learn
- we had to have working walls that had to be done the same way in every class
- we had no time to discuss workload because 'it is what it is at the moment and anyone should leave if they can't handle the pressure.'

- we should ensure we were 'happy' with the data we handed in otherwise there would be extra 'support' given to staff - massage data if needed?
- repeatedly in staff meetings, 'it's not a good picture'

Your stubborn and naive philosophy on how to improve the school meant you were completely blinkered to the good things that were already happening. There was nothing wrong with the children. There was nothing wrong with the staff. You had to prove your impact. The academy had to prove their impact. It was a hideous mess. Using the Ofsted's new focus on the curriculum, I am convinced the school would have been graded good or outstanding before your arrival. But sadly, for us, and perhaps for many other schools, that focus arrived too late. The hunger for good SATs results has been devastating.

Your obsession and appetite to raise SATs scores at any cost, has been at the expense of your teachers' well-being and pupils' mental health. Yes, the slightly improved SATs scores made you look good. It made the academy look good. But your curriculum sucked. Your ego was running the school. You seemed completely unaware of the damage your policies were causing.

I am very proud that I found the mental strength to leave your school. I am furious that so many teachers left due to stress and have never returned to the classroom. I have heard on the grapevine that you are now holding regular meetings in order to tackle the curriculum before Ofsted arrive. Good luck.

I thought I was the only one who had experienced this style of leadership. But apparently, it has become quite common in some schools. I wouldn't hesitate to resign again if my current school went down the same avenue. Luckily, they aren't. I am a much happier teacher, working in a happier school, managed by people who take well-being and workload seriously.

Fake Teacher

Secret Files No.1 - Praise

FHT: I noticed you only wrote praise for a lot of your pupils. Can you explain this?

Teacher: That's right. I know my children really well and they respond positively to praise.

FHT: But you don't have time to praise. Just write out next steps and more targets.

Teacher: But I give so much feedback within the lesson. I also give feedback to groups and individuals in the lesson. By the time I mark the work, they have received verbal feedback about ten times.

FHT: But if someone looks at your books, it looks like you haven't had any impact on that child?

Teacher: But it is clear I have because if you look back at their work several weeks ago, you can see a massive improvement. If the child has responded to my feedback and has put maximum effort into their work, I want to praise them. They have done everything I have asked of them. I am usually really proud of them.

FHT: I understand that, but we need to prove our impact. If I do a book scrutiny, how am I supposed to know the impact you have had?

Teacher: To be honest, I don't really care about the book scrutiny. Shouldn't good progress be the only thing that matters in a book scrutiny?

FHT: I think I am going to have to put you on a coaching program?

Teacher: What! But my class are doing so well. That's unfair.

FHT: But if we say we are writing next steps, setting daily targets, pinking and greening and using two stars and a wish every day, I need to see it in their books.

Teacher: I understand. I do those things when I can, if I think it's appropriate, but my real skill as a professional teacher is knowing when and how to give feedback within lessons.

FHT: Mmm.

Teacher: I'll get my coat.

Secret Files No.2 - Aldi

FHT: I hear many of you want to work at Aldi. I don't understand.

Teacher: Because I can turn up 5 minutes before I start, work hard and leave 5 minutes after I finish.

FHT: But won't you miss working with the children?

Teacher: Of course. I love teaching. But the job has changed significantly over the last few years and it's beginning to affect my well-being.

FHT: But what about the pay cut? You won't be able to afford to leave teaching! You are trapped.

Teacher: I know. It sucks. But I will get paid for the hours I work. If I work 50-60 hours a week at Aldi, I get paid for 50-60 hours. Currently I get paid 32.5 hours a week for working 50-60 hours.

FHT: But that's a very selfish attitude to take. It's a vocation.

Teacher: But I don't see my family and I haven't had a pay rise in years.

FHT: But we are under pressure to maintain our 'good' judgement. *'It is what it is,'* at the moment. It will get better.

Teacher: Can I go part time then?

FHT: No. I don't like part time teachers.

Teacher: Ok.

FHT: Where are you going?

Teacher: Aldi.

Secret Files No.3 - Evidence

FHT: I am surprised you've said some children have met objectives already on our on-line tracking tool. It's only October.

Teacher: That's because I know they can do it.

FHT: But our policy is to collect six pieces of evidence over the year before saying they've met an objective.

Teacher: But there's 150 objectives just for maths, reading and writing. You must trust me. If I feel they can do it, I will show they have met that objective on the online tracking tool.

FHT: But how do you know? Did you take photographs of their work and upload it to the online tracking tool?

Teacher: No. It's in their book.

FHT: But your tablet can take photos and it easy for you to upload things (once you've logged in, found the objective and remembered what to do). Everyone is doing it.

Teacher: But it's in their book and I spoke to them at length.

FHT: On six occasions?

Teacher: No. Some children just knew it before I started the unit. They explained the answer to a question in depth, showing a very good understanding. The objective was reading 3-digit numbers.

FHT: But did they really know? Can you prove it? Did you film them talking to you?

Teacher: Erm... no. Should I have done?

FHT: If you are saying they have met that objective, I think a short film uploaded to the online tracking tool would be great.

Teacher: But who looks at those videos?

FHT: Was it in a problem-solving situation?

Teacher: No. the objective just says, 'I can read 3-digit numbers'. He knew the value of each digit.

FHT: But everything must be mastery and reasoning.

Teacher: Yes. I understand but he can read 3-digit numbers confidently and shows a good understanding. He has met that objective.

FHT: But it's only October! The colours on the online tracking tool are supposed to change slowly and steadily over the year. This will mess around with my graphs.

Teacher: But he can do it!

FHT: I think you need some coaching.

Teacher: Bye.

FHT: Where are you going?

Teacher: I'm not sure anymore.

Secret Files No.4 - Proof of Impact

FHT: Thank you for welcoming me into your Requires Improvement school. I realise the previous Head was very popular but that is about to change. I am under enormous pressure to improve results here.

Teacher: Is that why you observed everyone in your first week?

FHT: Absolutely. I have to report back to my bosses who run hundreds of schools. I appreciate that most of you were given inadequate gradings. Sorry about that.

Teacher: But most of us are great teachers. Why didn't you just tell us what you wanted to see and then observe us in four weeks? It seems a little unfair. It feels like you are purposely catching us out.

FHT: I agree. I have to prove my impact to the bosses. If I make a baseline assessment of the teaching I see first, then I can tell you what to do to improve - whether you need to or not. After a term I can then tell my bosses what a difference I have made. In fact, I have already written on my action plan that 30% of you will be good again by the end of the summer term.

Teacher: That's a bit weird. So, is that why we have to test the children now every four weeks? To prove progress is happening.

FHT: Yes. Lots of testing. Proof of progress will keep me in a job.

Teacher: But it all seems a little excessive. I think it might turn children off learning and teachers off teaching? We only used to do formal testing three times a year. It was appropriate. Do you expect to see progress every four weeks from these tests? That's a lot of testing!

FHT: Yes. And if progress isn't seen, I will freeze your pay.

Teacher: Well. I know what teachers will start doing.

FHT: What's that?

Teacher: Never mind.

Secret Files No.5 - Verbal Feedback

FHT: Can I have a word?

Teacher: I really need to get home. The staff meeting over ran again by thirty minutes.

FHT: It is what it is at the moment. We must improve our data.

Teacher: Can we walk and talk then as I collect my things?

FHT: No, I'd rather go to my office.

Teacher: Oh. Alright then (gulp).

FHT: In my panic, I secretly looked at everyone's books at the weekend. I noticed that you are not using the verbal feedback stamper. Please explain.

Teacher: Oh. I thought I was in trouble.

FHT: You are.

Teacher: About not using the verbal feedback stamper?

FHT: Absolutely. You must use it every day to show you have given feedback to the class. This is in addition to any written feedback you give (which must be in the form of two stars and a wish every two days).

Teacher: But that's my job. I give verbal feedback (teaching) so many times in a lesson - to individuals and the whole class - I don't see the point in stamping 'Verbal Feedback Given' in their book. It's not something I even consider doing.

FHT: But it proves that you have given feedback. It shows Ofsted you have made a difference to that pupil.

Teacher: But look at the progress from this page to this page. You can clearly see the difference. You must assume I have taught well and used my professional judgement and expertise as appropriate. Ofsted don't care about what stampers I use.

FHT: Oh yes. I can see progress now you have pointed it out. I don't really look at that. I only look at my long list of things to check (stampers, highlighters, two stars and a wish etc.).

Teacher: Can I go now? I really must get home.

FHT: I have to be seen to be enforcing my policies so I will be putting you on an action plan. It looks good for Ofsted.

Teacher: What! I am a very experienced teacher. I have got a very difficult class working their socks off. Does that not count for anything anymore?

FHT: Not really. Please use the verbal feedback stamper.

Teacher: And you wonder why teachers are fed up.

FHT: Sorry, what was that?

Teacher: Nothing. Good night.

Secret Files No.6 - Finding Time

FHT: Can you explain why your medium and short-term planning wasn't uploaded to the server this week?

Teacher: Sorry, I am bit behind. I have been updating all my working walls you insist I do.

FHT: But the week before that I noticed you hadn't deep marked enough.

Teacher: Oh, that was because I was preparing for your two-hour pupil progress meeting.

FHT: But what about the week before that? You failed to attend any of the discos and other PTA events.

Teacher: Sorry. I was collecting evidence (and making some up) so you can be awarded the Diamond Kite Mark for 'We Are a Happy School' to put on your newsletters.

FHT: But that doesn't excuse the fact that you didn't type up, print and stick learning objective slips in all books for every lesson in the week before that.

Teacher: Oh, that was because I was mentoring an average student who was failing. I had to attend lots of other meetings.

FHT: But you were behind updating our expensive on-line tracking program the week before that.

Teacher: Oh, that was because I was writing up my medium and short-term plans that week.

FHT: But what about your working walls the week before that? They looked a bit out of date.

Teacher: I am so sorry about that. I was deep marking that week. Book scrutiny was coming up.

FHT: But that doesn't excuse the fact you hadn't prepared for the pupil progress meeting the week before that.

Teacher: That's because I was attending discos and other PTA events that week.

FHT: But what about all the evidence I had asked for the week before, so we can be awarded the Diamond Kite Mark for 'We Are a Happy School' so I can put them on our newsletters?

Teacher: Again, I am very sorry but that week I was concentrating on typing up learning objective slips for every lesson for every day.

FHT: But the week before that, you had failed to support the student properly.

Teacher: I know. I feel bad, but I was updating the hundreds of objectives on our expensive on-line tracking program that I know you love to look at.

FHT: Can you explain why your medium and short-term planning wasn't uploaded to the server the week before that?

Teacher: Sorry, I was a bit behind. That week, I was updating all my working walls you insist I do.

FHT: But the week before that I noticed you hadn't deep marked enough.

Teacher: Oh, that was because I was preparing for your two-hour pupil progress meeting.

FHT: But what about the week before that? You failed to attend any of the discos and PTA events.

Teacher: Sorry. I was collecting evidence (and making some up) so you can be awarded the diamond kite mark for 'We Are a Happy School' to put on your newsletters.

FHT: But that doesn't excuse the fact that you didn't type up, print and stick learning objective slips in all books for every lesson in the week before that.

Teacher: Oh, that was because I was mentoring an average student who was failing. I had to attend lots of other meetings.

FHT: But you were behind updating our expensive on-line tracking program the week before that.

Teacher: Oh, that was because I was writing up my medium and short-term plans that week.

FHT: But what about your working walls the week before that? They looked a bit out of date.

Teacher: I am so sorry about that. I was deep marking that week. Book scrutiny was coming up.

FHT: But that doesn't excuse the fact you hadn't prepared for the pupil progress meeting the week before that.

Teacher: That's because I was attending discos and other PTA events that week.

FHT: But what about all the evidence I had asked for the week before, so we can be awarded the Diamond Kite Mark for 'We Are a Happy School' so I can put them on our newsletters?

Teacher: Again, I am very sorry but that week I was concentrating on typing up learning objective slips for every lesson for every day.

FHT: But the week before that, you had failed to support the student properly.

Teacher: I know. I feel bad, but I was updating the hundreds of objectives on our expensive on-line tracking program that I know you love to look at.

FHT: Can you explain why your medium and short-term planning wasn't uploaded to the server the week before that?

Teacher: Sorry... shall we stop there?

Secret Files No.7 - That's Your Warning

FHT: I am giving you a written warning for not fully complying with my policies. It will last for twelve months and it will stay on your record.

Teacher: What! You have to be kidding? I was merely raising some of the problems staff have with some of your policies. I am a great teacher.

FHT: Yes, you are. But you are not fully supporting the school. You are causing too many problems. I expect you all to agree with everything I say.

Teacher: But I do on the whole. I had no idea these things were set in stone with little opportunity for discussion.

FHT: Sorry. It is what it is. I am under enormous pressure. You can appeal if you wish to.

Teacher: How do I do that?

FHT: Email me your appeal letter and I will forward it to my boss.

Teacher: Your boss? In the academy? That doesn't sound fair. She will agree with you.

FHT: No, of course she won't. She will be very professional.

Teacher: And what if she *does* agree with you? What happens then if I still feel your treatment of me is unfair?

FHT: You can appeal to *her* boss.

Teacher: The academy director?

FHT: Yes.

Teacher: I'm screwed then. Is it because I am too expensive, and you want to employ NQTs who will sign the new academy contract and save you thousands of pounds?

FHT: Don't be ridiculous. Of course not.

Teacher: So, the only way I can appeal against your decision to give me a written warning, that stays on my record (because I have questioned some of your policies), is to raise it with the academy?

FHT: Yes.

Teacher: So, let me get this straight. No third party gets involved who will look at the evidence objectively – apart from my union rep?

FHT: It all stays in house I'm afraid.

Teacher: Wow. I'm screwed then.

FHT: Yes. There's nothing you can do about it. Thanks for fifteen years of hard work.

Teacher: Hang on, that sounds like you have already decided that you want me to leave?

FHT: Don't be silly.

Teacher: But all the UPS3 teachers are on action plans now or off with stress because they have been burdened with too much work. Coincidence?

FHT: Are you questioning me again?

Teacher: Yes. I mean no. I don't know anymore. I just want to teach how I want to teach without following pages and pages of non-negotiables.

FHT: Right, let's make that an 18-month written warning.

Teacher: How many months can I stay off with stress at full pay?

FHT: Why do you ask?

I Just Want to Read My Book

My NQT year - twenty years ago.

Me: Your Year 4 class love reading!

Teacher: I know. My classes always love reading.

Me: How come?

Teacher: They just read after lunch every day.

Me: I do that too with my class.

Teacher: No, you don't. You look at a text with different groups and ask them lots of questions.

Me: But isn't that good teaching?

Teacher: Depends. That might help them confidently pass a reading test, but it won't inspire them to read.

Me: But I was told that silent reading isn't enough. Maybe on a Friday for a bit when no one is looking.

Teacher: How many children read at home? Honestly? How many parents read in front of their children? How many books are in the household? When is a child inspired to read?

Me: But I would feel guilty letting children read their own book every day.

Teacher: Really? Thirty minutes a day - in silence - with a book. That's 2.5 hours a week they have interrupted and quiet time to get lost in a book. Why do you feel bad?

Me: What are they learning though?

Teacher: Experience. To know what it feels like to want to read that book again and again. To build stamina and perseverance. To have an opportunity to read every day. To escape from the stresses and strains of everyday life for a bit. I don't really know but it works.

Me: But how do your children do in reading tests?

Teacher: Really well. It works, I don't know exactly but their love of reading definitely comes from being allowed to read every day. I listen to them read too.

Me: It's that easy?

Teacher: Yup!

Me: I'm going to do that then!

I did this every day for several years. It worked! But then I was told I had to teach reading in small groups and ask lots of questions about every page. I had to start collecting evidence for moderation meetings. It wasn't the same. Shame.

Letter to My Friend

Dear Friend,

I hope you are well. I have some interesting news to share with you.

Do you remember I was asked to lead that Requires Improvement School? The academy trust gave me a huge pay rise of over 125k a year. They told me exactly what to do and how to do it. So, I did.

I had only taught for five years before becoming a super Head, so I used all my teaching experience to try and turn the school around. As you know, 20% of the staff left in the first year. That was understandable. Dead wood. Too expensive.

To make things easier for staff, I introduced pages of non-negotiables and conformance and consistency policies. It worked in my last school, 200 miles away, so I was confident it would work here too. Granted, the catchment and demographics were completely different.

To my surprise, staff have had unions in complaining about my draconian management style. Since September, six teachers have been on long term sickness absence and another four teachers are resigning at Christmas.

According to my PA, another twelve teachers are thinking of leaving before they are forced out or too anxious to teach anymore.

Some say I don't have what it takes. Some say I lack empathy. Some say I am only interested in data and I don't invest in developing relationships with the staff and pupils. Perhaps they are right.

I found out last night that our academy trust has been told to leave the school. My impact on the school hasn't been good enough. So, it looks like I will be losing my job after Christmas. I'll be alright though because I am so arrogant. I'll bounce back immediately. They will move me silently into another job with a similar wage packet.

One of the teachers said it wasn't fair that I had negatively affected the mental health and careers of so many good teachers, only to be sacked myself. She's probably right. Some might say how tragic this is. Apparently, it has happened in a lot of schools.

They need to toughen up a bit I say. I am already looking forward to my next challenge. I have a two-year plan. If I do well, I will move up the pay scale very quickly. If I don't, and ruin it all for everyone again, I will be moved on again.

Anyway, say hi to the family.

See you soon,

Fake Headteacher

I Don't Want to Be Told

I don't want to be told how to teach writing.

I don't want to be told how to teach maths.

I don't want to be told how to teach reading.

I don't want to be told when best to teach particular lessons.

I don't want to be told what resources I must be seen to be using.

I don't want to be told what colour pen to use.

I don't want to be told how to give written feedback.

I don't want to be told how often I should give written feedback.

I don't want to be told to use a verbal feedback stamper whenever I help a pupil.

I don't want to be told to use any stampers for that matter.

I don't want to be told how pupils should peer assess.

I don't want to be told how often pupils need to peer assess.

I don't want to be told how many static displays I can have.

I don't want to be told how many working walls I must have.

I don't want to be told what needs to be seen on my working walls.

I don't want to be told whether I should type or handwrite titles on displays.

I don't want to be told how work should be mounted.

I don't want to be told how my PowerPoints and flipcharts should look.

I don't want to be told to type up learning objective slips with 5 success criteria bullet points on - for every lesson, that need to be printed and stuck in books.

I don't want to be told to highlight, initial or tick learning objective slips after the lesson to show the pupil if they 'got it'.

I don't want to tell pupils to blindly tick learning objective slips to tell me how they felt about their learning.

I don't want to be told my books are being scrutinised again, and again and again.

I don't want to be told that one pupil didn't underline their date on Tuesday.

I don't want to be told I missed a pupil's spelling mistake.

I don't want to be told learning walks will be carried out every week.

I don't want to be told to expect unannounced learning walks any day which make me anxious every night so I work more than I should.

I don't want to be told my pupils must make more progress than is probably possible.

I don't want to be told half my class will miss their favourite lessons in the afternoon because they must attend booster groups.

I don't want to be told that lunchtime has been shortened to cram in more learning in the afternoon.

I don't want to be told to attend pointless Monday morning briefings for twenty minutes when I should be preparing my lessons.

I don't want to be told staff meetings will now last 2 hours.

I don't want to be told how often to assess.

I don't want to be told how to evidence assessment for learning.

I don't want to be told I am being given extra responsibilities simply because I moved to UPS1.

I don't want to be told I am too negative when I challenge an idea put forward.

I don't want to be told 'don't stay too late' when I am trying to keep up with workload you have created.

I don't want to be told what topics I must teach and when.

I don't want to be told 'have a lovely weekend,' when you know I will be working on Sunday.

I don't want to be told how I must plan lessons.

I don't want to be told what planning templates I must use.

I don't want to be told how my furniture should be arranged.

I don't want to be told I can't go to my daughter's sports day.

I don't want to be told what highlighters I must use to give feedback.

I don't want to be told to tell pupils they are below the national average for their age when they are only seven.

I don't want to be told what colour paper certain pieces of work must go on.

I don't want to be told how disappointed you were that I couldn't attend the school fair and only volunteered to run one club for two terms.

I don't want to be told practical lessons must be evidenced in books with photos and annotations.

I don't want to be told we need to improve anymore.

I don't want to be told, 'It is what it is.'

I don't want to be told the workload will ease off after we get an outstanding grade.

I don't want to be told pupil premium pupils must show excellent progress.

I don't want to be told that pupil premium children must attend interventions even if they don't need to.

I don't want to be told to concentrate on pupils who might make end of year expectations and ignore the poor ones - all to make data look good.

I don't want to be told to bend the rules when administering tests and assessments.

I don't want to be told to 'nudge' written assessment up a little.

I don't want to be told my salary is being frozen because pupil grades were not good enough based on inflated predictions.

I don't want to work at home every night trying to keep up with the minimum required.

I don't want to be told that I have 36 pupils in my class next year.

I don't want to see colleagues upset and feeling demotivated anymore.

I don't want to see good teachers leaving teaching anymore.

I don't want to be told my class are making good progress, but I still need to conform to all the non-negotiables that are now in place or else.

I just want to be trusted to do what I am good at, even if it's not the same as my colleagues.

I want to use all my experience, expertise and training to teach to the best of my ability.

I don't want to feel boxed in and stifled by strict policies that remove autonomy.

I don't want to be constantly told how to do my job and suffer serious consequences when I don't.

I don't want to be told anymore.

I really don't.

Interview Questions

End of interview questions:

'Well that's everything from us. Do you have any questions you would like to ask the panel?

'Yes please. How do you want me to teach maths? How have you interpreted maths mastery and how do you want me to do it?

How do you want me to teach literacy? How do you want me to teach reading?

How many pens and highlighters do I have to use?

What colour must my PowerPoint slides be?

What comments should I write in their books and how often?

Am I allowed to write praise in books?

How often do you carry out book scrutinies?

How long is the non-negotiables list for book scrutinies?

Do I type, print and stick in learning objective slips?

How many other things need to be on the slip?

Will I have my own trimmer? Do you have funds for an endless supply of glue sticks?

Do I need to use stampers?

Do I have to write 'Verbal feedback given' every time I talk to a pupil?

Do your half-termly assessments bear any relation to the work we actually cover?

How often do I attend pupil progress meetings? What happens to me if a pupil hasn't made enough progress?

Will I still get paid if some pupils don't make enough progress?

Am I allowed to give stickers out?

What tracking software do you use? How many hundreds of objectives do I need to update and how often?

How should I ask questions to class? Lolly sticks, hands up, no hands up?

What colour pen do pupils edit in? How often do you need to see evidence of peer feedback? What should it look like?

How should I write the letters k, f, x, z? What letters are not joined?

What should my displays look like? Are they *all* working walls? What are the non-negotiables for displays? When do you inspect them?

Please tell me you mostly look for progress in books.

Can I group children how I want to, on a day to day basis, or do you tell me how to group them?

Do I have to use random chat chums? How often do they change?

Are learning walks designed to help me improve or as a way of policing consistency policies?

How often do you drop into lessons and what happens if you see something you don't like?

How much autonomy will I have? If any?

Will you support me with poor behaviour from a pupil or tell me my lessons need to improve?

Are you aware of current education trends? Do you use research to help improve the school?

Do you have an edu-twitter account?

Do you use phrases like 'It is what it is' and 'We have to play the game' to justify your policies?

Do all classrooms have to look the same?

Do staff feel like robots?

What's the atmosphere like in school?

How are you addressing workload?

Is your school a SATs factory or do you have a broad and balanced curriculum?

Are teachers happy here? Are *you* happy here?

Erm...I think that's it. I didn't get the job, did I? I'll get my coat.

Thanks for the opportunity.'

I Feel Sick

I am in my third year of teaching.

I feel sick.

I am sitting at a pupil's desk.

In front of me are thirty books that need to be 'deep marked'.

I have to deep mark twice a week apparently.

I will need to highlight bits I like in green. I will need to highlight bits in pink to show where pupils need to improve.

In addition, I will need to write a couple of next steps that pupils must respond to. But that's ok because we now have 'feedback to learning' time built into our timetables - thirty minutes after lunch. We don't do quiet reading now.

I feel sick.

I feel sick because I know I have already given so much feedback to all thirty pupils in the lesson.

Nearly every pupil has responded to my advice. Nearly every pupil has made progress and moved forward with their learning.

The only thing I want to do, is to write a congratulatory comment.

They deserve it. They did everything I asked of them. A lovely comment will motivate them and reward their hard work.

But I know that I have to deep mark twice a week and it's already Wednesday.

I will need to highlight bits I like in green. I will need to highlight bits in pink to show pupils where they need to improve. I will need to write a couple of next steps.

I don't want to.

It's common sense to me.

I already knew from the previous lesson what to teach today. I discussed the lesson with my TA afterwards and had a flick through the books to double check how they got on.

I made a few notes on whole class misconceptions or things they found a bit wobbly.

I wrote down a couple of new things I wanted to introduce too.

I made notes on the few who struggled and the few who needed extending.

I had a quick chat with the pupils who struggled yesterday, just before the lesson today, to give them a bit of a boost.

I started the lesson showing pupils examples of misconceptions from yesterday.

I used the visualiser to help improve an actual piece of work from one of the pupils. I gave time for all pupils to re-address this in the lesson.

I taught the new skills for the lesson.

I checked their understanding throughout the lesson and stopped the lesson if I thought I needed to re-address anything.

I quickly picked up on individual errors and supported them in a variety of ways.

I extended my more able (based on yesterday's lesson) with questions and challenges such as 'Can you now...? Show me' etc.

I stopped the lesson to look at good examples of work and discussed ways we could move the learning further forward.

I gave opportunities for pairs to evaluate each other's work and respond accordingly.

I lost count the about of times I gave advice or fed-back to individuals, groups or the whole class.

We shared some work at the end and congratulated each other on our successes.

I gave some last-minute bits of advice for the pupils to think about.

I have just flicked through books and made notes for tomorrow.

But...

I am still sitting at a pupil's desk.

In front of me are thirty books that still need to be 'deep marked'.

I have to deep mark twice a week.

I will need to highlight bits I like in green. I will need to highlight bits in pink to show pupils what to improve.

In addition, I will need to write a couple of next steps that pupils must respond to.

I better crack on.

Come On. Keep Up!

- Accountability
- Action plans
- Anxiety
- Assessment for learning
- Assessments
- Autonomy
- Behaviour
- Book looks
- Book scrutiny
- Break duties
- Capabilities
- Challenge
- Class assemblies
- Class blogs
- Class newsletters
- Class twitter page
- Coaching
- Cognitive load
- Cold tasks
- Concrete methods
- Conjunctions
- Consistency
- Correct PowerPoint colours
- Cross-curricular
- Curriculum
- Data
- Deep dive
- Deep mark
- Differentiation
- Emails
- Evidence
- Exceeding
- Exception words
- Explain your thinking

- Fluency
- Fronted adverbials
- Glue sticks
- Good Ofsted
- Growth mindset
- Highlighter pens
- Homework
- Hot tasks
- Independence
- Individual learning plans
- Inspection
- Interventions
- Learners
- Logins
- Long date
- Marking codes
- Mastery
- Meeting standards
- Meetings
- Mentoring
- Middle management
- Mini plenaries
- Modal verbs
- Modelling
- Moderation
- More able
- Next steps
- Non-negotiables
- Nrich
- Objectives
- Observation feedback
- Observations
- Ofsted
- On track
- Outstanding Ofsted
- Pace
- Parent workshops

- Passwords
- Peer feedback
- Performance management
- Phone calls
- Photos
- Pictorial method
- Planned learning walks
- Planning
- Plenaries
- Printing
- Proof of impact
- Prove it
- Pupil progress
- Purple pens
- Questions
- Random pairs
- Rapid graspers
- Raw scores
- Requires improvement
- Risk assessments
- Safeguarding
- Same day interventions
- SATs
- Scaffolding
- Short date
- Stampers
- Standardised scores
- Star of the week
- Stem
- Success criteria
- Support program
- Teacher feedback
- Toolkits
- Tracking
- Trimming
- Trips
- Twilights

- Twinkl
- Two stars and a wish
- Typed up learning objectives
- Unannounced learning walks
- Verbal feedback
- Videos
- Visual timetables
- Visualiser
- Well-being
- Working walls
- Workload

How Are Your Plants?

Plant Inspector:

Why have your plants not met national standards in plant growth?

Daytime Plant Carer:

We can only work with what we are given. Most of our plants we inherit are so far behind. The plant shop down the road are lucky. They seem to inherit the best plants that arrive on day one, in their own pots and are already doing very well. It's easier for that plant shop.

Plant Inspector:

Everyone says that to me!

It makes no difference what plant you are given in the first place. Your plants must meet national standards. I am afraid I am grading your shop 'requires improvement' based on your plant growth during their first few year's growth in your shop.

Daytime Plant Carer:

But we have no control over our night-time plant carers. We can only do so much. The plant shop down the road have superior night-time carers. We simply can't compete with them.

We have some of the most hard-working daytime plant carers you'll ever see. They regularly go above and beyond what is expected from them. It's not fair.

Plant Inspector:

Tough. See you soon!

But You Get All the Holidays!

Billy works in an office. He is talking to his teacher friend.

But you get all those paid holidays! Lucky you.

> We do but our salary is spread out over the year. It's complicated. But yes, the holidays are a time to connect with my friends and family again.

How many weeks holiday do you get again?

> About 13 weeks.

And you get paid for those weeks?

> Well no. But yes. Most people get 4 weeks off a year. So, if you take that away, that only leaves 9 weeks holiday I suppose.

Are you having a laugh! Is that supposed to make me feel better! Ha, ha. 9 weeks! So that's 32.5 hours a week multiplied by 9 weeks…. That's 292 hours you get paid for doing nothing!

> Actually, I get paid 32.5 hours a week, 39 weeks a year (not including holiday pay). But I work 60 hours a week. So, I work 1,267 hours extra. It's not paid overtime. I must work these hours in order to keep up with the demands of the job. The number is actually higher than that because we often work in the holidays too. So yes, I am paid in the holidays but…. do the maths.

Oh. I didn't realise.

No. Not many people do. In fact, I don't get paid for holiday time. My salary is spread out over the year. Now, I must get on with some schoolwork. I'll speak soon.

But it's Sunday!

Yup!

I Need to See a Doctor

I'm having terrible nightmares at the moment. In my dream, I have an extremely positive conversation with staff at my new school. It's the same conversation every night. It's truly awful. It's affecting my sleep. They go something like this...

'First thing's first. You may mark books with any colour pen. It makes no difference to learning.

Pupils can improve their work with pencil or pen, in any colour you decide. They will still improve. There's no need to evidence editing with a purple pen.

You can write what you like in books – or write nothing at all. As long as feedback occurs. That goes without saying - you are a teacher after all. That's what you do all day. You probably give feedback all the time!

I don't usually carry out book scrutinies. I thought we could just share some books in a staff meeting to see what everyone else is up to. It will be great to share some good work together. I know you work hard to ensure books look nice. That's why you like teaching. I know you'll want pupils to present work neatly etc. It's second nature for you. You don't need me to give you a long set of 'book rules' to adhere to. It'll be like you're at school again... oh hang on. You know what I mean!

We do have a school reward system, but you can do your own thing too as each class responds differently. Make it work for you and your class.

If ever you need me to talk to any pupil about their behaviour, please let me know. It can be tough at times and a stern, but supportive word with a pupil from me can go a long way. Please use me as your back up. You don't need to worry. It has nothing to do with your teaching. I will phone parents for you too if needed.

If you want me to see you teach and give you any pointers on how you could improve, then great. If not, I see no reason to pop in at all. I'll leave it up to you. Learning walks are not particularly positive experiences for anyone. You'll just put on a show for me anyway. It's not normal. I won't see you naturally teach. I trust you. I assume you have a teaching qualification!

In addition, every time someone visits our school, I promise not to use it as an opportunity to carry out a learning walk. Not that I do them anyway.

Tests will be kept to a minimum and will only test content you have taught. I am not interested in giving tests just to collect data using test papers that often assess parts of the curriculum not yet taught.

You know full well how to help and support children, so I see no need to take you out of class to attend pupil progress meetings. I trust you to do your best. I know you will tell me if you have any concerns. You only teach pupils for a few hours a day and I fully appreciate how their home life affects their learning and overall performance. I simply refuse to hold you fully accountable if a pupil doesn't make accelerated progress - especially if you have done your best.

I don't do morning diary meetings. Sorry! I will write bits and bobs on the staffroom whiteboard. You can read it in your own time.

You can share the learning objective with pupils how you see fit. If you want pupils to write it fully in books you can, or even just a one-word title will suffice. Type them up if you want to but there really is no need. Or, write one on the white board and just have it displayed during the lesson. Pupils don't even need to write it out then. I don't really mind either way - it has the same impact on the learning. It's not really up to me to tell you how to share the learning objective. Do what works for you.

Please use your display boards how you see fit. Working walls or static boards are fine with me. You know your class better than anyone. You know the level of support and visual stimulation they need. I trust you. I won't be checking. You have loads of ideas that are way better than mine anyway!

If you want to run a club, that's great. But you'll have other priorities so concentrate on those first. There's no expectation to run clubs.

UPS staff. Thank you from the bottom of my heart for sticking with teaching and continuing to set a good example to others. I value you so much. You make your job look easy but that doesn't mean I need to give you extra responsibilities. That was never the idea. You deserve that extra bit of money. Your experience is invaluable. Thank you for challenging me and keeping me on my toes. Thank you again.

I will email you when I need to, certainly not in the evenings or at weekends. That's the right thing to do to keep anxiety levels to a minimum.

I will allocate an inset day for report writing and four staff meetings. I know it's not much, but it should help.

We have bought in schemes for literacy and maths but if you have your own methods based on your own experience and research then please do that instead - I wouldn't want to suffocate your own strengths and skill sets. However, we may ask you to use the schemes if we have concerns about your teaching. In most cases, you will have full autonomy to choose what's best for you and your class.

School policies will be called 'school policies' – not non-negotiables. That term is banned. It sounds too serious.

Please feel free to mark books during lessons if children are independently working. There are times when you absolutely must do this to catch up, or to work 1:1 with pupils as you come across their misconceptions. I won't criticise you for this at all. It's your job after all. You decide.

I will always provide lunch for inset days. It's the very least I can do. You work so hard all year. I also won't charge for tea and coffee - another perk you should be able to enjoy.

There's no need to update blogs and upload everything to the website every week. Perhaps upload a few photos at the end of term. Other than that, use the time saved to concentrate on lessons. That must be your focus.

Every teacher will have enough glue sticks. Always. They play a significant part in your day. It's a no brainier for me and will help to reduce stress. No need for your TA to hoard them anymore.

All classes will have a trimmer. End of. They're cheap enough.

You can photocopy in colour. It helps to make lessons more engaging and makes things look a bit nicer.

I have already paid for a school Twinkl account so there's no need to pay for it out of your own money.

Please remember to give your receipts for anything you buy out of your own money to improve lessons. The bursar will happily reimburse you. I hope that's ok.

Teaching is hard enough without having to be told you must stay at school during PPA. You are allowed to work at home (or just have some time for yourself). I realise you work long hours all the time. I wish I could give you more PPA to be honest. Half a day is so inadequate.

Staff meetings are every week unless I can see your workload increasing. In which case, I might give you a couple of staff meetings off. I will finish at 4:30 without fail. I have stuff to do too. It's just nice to touch base every week and discuss and share some ideas. They won't be used to criticise you or to roll out initiative after initiative. Who likes doughnuts by the way?

Anything related to school policies or data, will only go up in the PPA room. The staff room should be a place to switch off. I have some Monet prints I could put up instead, but I am open to suggestions.

I will reinstate afternoon breaks. It's so important that pupils get ten minutes in the afternoon to run around. It's when they are most fidgety. It makes perfect sense. You can sort out your next lesson or go to the loo! I am happy to be on duty during this time.

I have overviews for the year, so I don't need to see medium-term plans or daily annotated plans to check you are teaching properly.

I promise not to become best friends with any member of staff. It's important I keep a professional distance from you all. It gets awkward otherwise. I hope you understand. I have my own group of friends anyway out of school and don't need to attach myself to a small group of teachers who kiss my butt all day. I just want to be fair and treat everyone honestly.

I am not interested in winning kite mark awards. They create extra work for staff. They're used to put on the bottom of letters to parents. It's not worth it if you have to spend so much time collecting evidence for them. Is that ok with you? Parents won't notice anyway.

Parents will not have access to staff email addresses. Emails will be filtered appropriately via the office staff. Is that ok?

I have reinstated the staff toilets, so you don't have to use the same ones as the pupils. I understand the theory behind sharing but it's not pleasant. They are pretty grim eh. You deserve to be able to go to the loo without pupils standing outside the door listening in.

I am sure there a few other things I have forgotten. I will let you know in due course. In the meantime, have a great day.'

I may need to see the doctor. It's really affected me. Such a bad dream.

Fake Headteacher

Hang On. I Used to be Good

Lesson observation:

Something is criticised. Teacher told to improve. An additional observation is planned.

Next lesson observation:

Teacher feels anxious.

Something else is criticised. Written support plan issued. Additional observations are planned. Teacher starts to over think things.

Next lesson observation:

Teacher hasn't slept well for days. Teacher feels very anxious. Teacher teaches unnaturally trying to tick all the boxes observer expects to see. Lesson feels awkward. Pupils pick up on teacher anxiety. Teacher spends more time listening to observer grilling pupils about their learning. Teacher watches observer write notes on their clipboard after every sentence teacher says. Observer looks through books and makes more notes. Once again, aspects of lesson are criticised. New things.

Next lesson observation:

This lesson *has* to be good. Capability procedure has been threatened. Teacher hasn't slept properly for weeks. Teacher feels very confused because they have a history of great teaching. Teacher doesn't know if they're coming or going. Teacher isn't teaching how they want to anymore. Teacher knows deep down that the lesson won't go well. Other teachers have told the teacher they are being targeted unfairly. Teacher refuses to believe this but the teacher is on UPS and about to reach their 45th birthday, so maybe.

Lesson doesn't go well. Teaching assistant cries because she thought lesson was great. Staff are panicking now because they don't want to go through same experience.

Next lesson observation:

Doesn't happen. Teacher now off long-term sick. Teacher resigns. NQT appointed.

The Ten Second Game

Time for something completely different!

This game is brilliant. I created it many years ago and the children love it. Great for the end of term. Have fun!

Ten Second game:

1. Choose someone to play.

2. Quickly countdown '3-2-1 go'

3. Pupil counts to ten seconds in their head and teacher starts stopwatch.

4. Pupil shouts out 'stop' when they think they have got to ten seconds.

5. Teacher stops stopwatch and tells them their time. e.g. 8.67 seconds.

6. Write name and time on board

7. If anyone stops the stopwatch on exactly 10.00 seconds, teacher has to reward the class with something nice.

Additional rules:

A) no watches or clocks to be looked at by pupils.

B) game must be done in silence.

C) if anyone talks when someone is counting, the pupil has another go and if they stop it on ten seconds, that pupil gets an extra reward, taken from the person who was talking during their turn. Stops pupils talking!

D) perhaps have a reward for pupil closest to ten seconds.

Adapt game to suit.

Enjoy!

NQT Definition Guide

NQT definition guide:

Even better if

How someone else would do it. It might be different, but not necessarily better. Leaders must be seen to be improving the school. Just go with it as best you can. It's not personal.

Non-negotiable

A made-up term to bully staff into teaching and marking in a particular way. It's not always the best way, or based on research, or suits your preferred way of managing your class but be careful, if you don't do them, you'll be quickly put on a support plan.

'It is what it is.'

A phrase, leaders use to bounce away comments about workload and well-being. It's usually to do with the pressures leading up to an Ofsted inspection. Promises will made that after an Ofsted visit, concerns about workload will be addressed. Often, it's not.

'After Ofsted, things will ease off.'

No. Not usually. The increased workload to achieve the improved Ofsted grade will stay the same, as leaders will think that the pages of non-negotiables worked. They won't let that drop now. Sorry.

Mastery

I'm still not sure what it means. Everyone has interpreted this differently. Everyone does the same. Extend by showing mastery? Just nod politely when mastery is mentioned. Tell your friends you teach maths mastery. They will be impressed. Hopefully, they won't ask you to go into detail.

Book Scrutiny

Every few weeks, leaders will check you're using the right pen to mark with, learning objectives are presented in the correct manner, pupils are using a ruler, pupils are using purple pens, the correct number of next steps are written by the teacher etc. It's a ball ache. The adverts don't mention any of this. If you're lucky, leaders will look at whether pupils are making progress regardless. If you're lucky.

Learning Walks

You don't learn anything. Pupils don't learn anything. It's a poorly named phrase. Think of it as a conformance walk. Are you conforming to the long list of things they expect to see? During the ten minutes they pop in, have a sip of your Red Bull and perform like a rock star. You'll be fine. Have the non-negotiables list displayed somewhere so you can quickly refer to it when you get very nervous. Expect lots of negative feedback. Leaders are under a lot of pressure.

UPS

UPS – upper pay scale. Looks good on paper. The idea was to reward good teachers who wanted to stay in teaching but not necessarily wanting to become senior managers. Ha, ha. Nowadays, schools can't afford to keep staff on UPS, so they have overloaded them with extra work in the hope they will resign. Often UPS staff are bullied into leaving. NQTs like yourself are so much cheaper and will conform immediately in most cases. Don't move onto UPS. It's not as good as it looks.

Pupil Progress Meetings

You'll love these. Every half-term, you will be interrogated by a member of the SLT. They will want to know how you intend to teach your class. They will want to know how you will help the pupils. They will want to know what you will do about pupils who are not making progress. Expect them to give you unrealistic targets for the pupils to meet. This is the start of the accountability pressure. Get used to it.

Working Walls

Don't waste your time coming in over the holidays to create beautiful displays. Working walls are the new thing. Slap sheets up on them as you go. Hand write everything. The messier they look, the better. Make them look raw, edgy and current. You will need to update them every day to prove learning is thriving in your classroom. You'll get bored very quickly, but you must keep all the working walls up to date. They will check. You won't have much choice I am afraid. Every classroom will look the same. Sorry.

Verbal Feedback

Basically, verbal feedback is whenever you tell a pupil how to improve. Leaders want evidence of this now. I know it's your job, but everything must be proven. So, whenever you help a pupil, make sure you write VF on the book and annotate it explaining what you said. Alternatively, get a verbal feedback stamper. Of course, you give feedback all the time in lessons but just play the game. Write one VF every day to keep leaders off your back.

Good luck!

I Have Resigned. Why?

Maybe, Perhaps, Probably.

After twenty-two years teaching in primary schools, I resigned this summer. I am 44. I am a good teacher. I love teaching so what went wrong?

Maybe I am just burnt out? Perhaps teaching full-time for twenty-two years takes its toll on us? I wonder if we struggle more with our mental health the longer we stay in the classroom?

Maybe having my own children (who are at primary school) has created a conflict of interest and I now find it hard to balance the two. Perhaps I spend more time thinking about the children at school than my own children? Actually, I know I do.

Maybe I worry about how teaching is affecting my mental and physical health. Perhaps leaving teaching will have a massive, positive effect on my well-being and overall happiness.

Maybe I want to feel like I've had a good night's sleep? Perhaps my mental 'to do list' is too overwhelming at times and creates unnecessary anxiety?

Maybe I crave to have more time to invest in myself, friends and family instead of doing schoolwork most nights at home. Perhaps I want to enjoy Sundays with my family without thinking about all the work I need to cram in at some point during the day?

Maybe going through a personal family tragedy has somehow affected my priorities and no longer care as much about certain aspects of the job? Perhaps it has put aspects of the job more into perspective and I've realised it's only a job - a job that is too hard to sustain at the levels expected without encroaching on time at home.

Maybe it's because I tire more easily as I've become older? Perhaps I just don't have the same level of energy and 'get up and go' as I used to and that affects my day to day enthusiasm?

Maybe I am fed up with being micro-managed to such a point, it feels suffocating? Perhaps the lack of trust and autonomy has simply demotivated me?

Maybe I don't like being told how to use my display boards and how and when to mark books? Perhaps I am fed up with countless learning walks and observations where I must be seen to be doing particular things SLT want to see?

Maybe I am tired of being told progress is too slow or not good enough and then interrogated in pupil progress meetings, grilling me as to what I am doing about it? Perhaps I am angry that pupil progress is mostly about data from countless tests?

Maybe it was because a particular Headteacher destroyed the confidence of many teachers at one school I worked at (all had a proven track record of good teaching) because he was under pressure to show his impact? Perhaps I never recovered from that experience and I am still shocked that schools could be run like this?

Maybe I am fed up of being told what fads SLT want to see in lessons followed by the inevitable feedback on how to do them better? (most of which are not based on research or years of experience). Perhaps I feel confused as to what I should be doing in lessons now and feel restricted in how I want to deliver lessons naturally?

Maybe I don't want to use particular coloured slides or resources that we have to use? Perhaps I don't want to follow a particular scheme of work because it's poor, but I am told I have to?

Maybe I find the introduction of initiative after initiative a little tedious now? Perhaps I've seen it all before and just want to be able to use my professional judgement?

Maybe I don't want my books to be scrutinised every few weeks to see if I am following the book non-negotiables? Perhaps I want SLT to look at the progress first and congratulate me on my teaching rather than on how often I have deep marked and what colour pens I use?

Maybe I just don't have the same patience dealing with challenging behaviour from pupils? Perhaps I want to feel more respected and supported by parents?

Maybe I am too expensive to move schools? Perhaps UPS teachers are being made to feel like they're not good enough and feel under pressure to leave?

I'm not sure if it's any of those things in particular. I wonder if it's a culmination of all of them? Probably.

I was recently asked what would need to happen for me to return to teaching? I thought about it for a few seconds. This is what I said:

Complete autonomy over how I mark and give feedback to pupils.

For progress to be the only thing a book scrutiny looks at – and less of them!

Complete autonomy over how I want to use my display boards and how I present my learning environment.

To have the freedom to use my experience in the classroom and knowledge gained from research to deliver lessons how I see fit. I don't want to be told what lessons must look like.

Why does consistency mean everyone does the same? I want the freedom to branch off.

I want to sit pupils how I want to.

I want to feel trusted and respected as a teacher. Learning walks and unannounced drop ins have become excessive. Back off.

There are signs that schools are beginning to change (my recent school especially) but for the moment, I need to recharge and reinvest in myself and my own family before I entertain the idea of returning. If at all.

Teacher

ωTF

Parent: Thanks for leaving books out to peruse during parents evening. I don't understand some of the marking. Can you explain what VF means?

Teacher: Of course. No problem. VF is written or stamped next to your child's work if an adult has suggested an idea or helped them in anyway.

Parent: So basically, if you speak to my child you have to write VF to prove you have spoken to them.

Teacher: Erm. Yes. It's a book scrutiny thing.

Parent: A what? What's that?

Teacher: The management team regularly look at the children's books to check we are writing VF so many times a week – amongst a whole load of other things.

Parent: Wtf. That's weird. Don't they trust you? Why on earth do you need to write VF every time you speak to my child about his work? Also, why have you highlighted some of his work in green and pink?

Teacher: Oh, that's to show your child the bits I liked and the bits he needs to improve.

Parent: Why don't you just tick the bits you like? Must be quicker than repeatedly picking up a variety of pens when marking.

Teacher: I would love to just tick good bits - even double tick! I am not allowed to though. It must be a green highlighter.

Parent: That's nuts! So, you don't have a choice?

Teacher: I'm afraid not.

Parent: Has anyone asked if the children mind teachers highlighting their work in different colours? That would have annoyed me at school.

Teacher: I don't think so. It's a good point!

Parent: I noticed that every page has a learning objective slip with a success criterion and feedback faces for pupils to colour in. They must cost a lot to buy in.

Teacher: Not really. We create them ourselves. I have to type them up every day, print them off, trim them and get pupils to stick them in with the four glue sticks we have left.

Parent: Wtf. Seriously? Why? That must take ages to do each week and for what reason?

Teacher: So the children know what they are learning. It makes books look good for Ofsted. We do them for every lesson, every day.

Parent: Can't you just tell them what they are learning about or get children to write a very simple 1-2 word title? Surely Ofsted don't care about this.

Teacher: It's a non-negotiable. I must do them.

Parent: Wtf. A non- what? That's nuts. When do you get time to do all this nonsense? You must have other priorities?

Teacher: Of course, but I'll get put on a support plan if I don't do what I am told to do.

Parent: Why do you have to draw little ladders and stars and wishes in books? Don't tell me they're non-negotiable?

Teacher: Little ladders are to let the child know they have a next step – I write a next step comment next to the ladder. The ladder makes it obvious where the next step comment is located. Stars are drawn to show where the pupil can find a positive comment. And a wand (wish) shows them where to find another moving on comment. And yes, they are non-negotiables.

Parent: That's ludicrous. Can't you just tell the children? Why do you need to write it all out for every child? Must take you hours.

Teacher: Yes. Yes, it does. I suppose you want to know why I have written SDI next to your child's work too?

Parent: Absolutely. Looks a bit rude – like he has an infection!

Teacher: Well, if I feel your child needs extra support, I am not allowed to help him in the next lesson. Instead, he must miss his afternoon lessons and attend a same day intervention group with four other children. To evidence this happened, I must write SDI his book. Sometimes I forget to write it in and have to spend all weekend writing all these codes and symbols in books, so I don't get told off.

Parent: Wtf. So, you retrospectively add comments and draw symbols etc., if you feel it will help keep the management off your back.

Teacher: Yes. Sad eh. It's just not worth the hassle. Most things I write in books isn't for the child.

Parent: What do you mean?

Teacher: It's to please a slightly obsessive management team who like to micro-manage people. They must prove their impact, I guess.

Parent:

Teacher: Are you ok? What's wrong?

Parent:

Teacher: Can I get you a glass of water?

Parent: Are all schools like this?

Teacher: Apparently not. Some schools are trying really hard to reduce workload and to minimise marking and non-negotiables.

Parent: Why don't you move schools?

Teacher: Actually, I have just resigned. The job has become too hard at present. When I am trusted to do the job I trained for and have a certain amount of autonomy, I may come back.

Parent: But you're an amazing teacher with years of experience.

Teacher: Yup.

Parent: Wtf.

I Don't Want to Work in an Outstanding School

What's the workload and general well-being like in your school?

Outstanding school:

It's good
It's bearable
Could be better
Terrible

Good school:

It's good
It's bearable
Could be better
Terrible

Requires Improvement school:

It's good
It's bearable
Could be better
Terrible

Inadequate school:

It's good
It's bearable
Could be better
Terrible

It's not the Ofsted grading that determines workload and well-being at your school, it's how your SLT decides to manage the grading. I have worked in a couple of Requires Improvement schools which had happy staff with a great work-life balance. I have worked in Good schools where the atmosphere was terrible, and the workload was off the scale.

Job Interviews Are Changing

Dear Head / Governors,

I am interested in the position of class teacher at your school.

I will be arriving at your school on the date suggested, to interview you and your SLT.

In particular, I will be focusing on work life balance, marking, learning walks, use of displays and accountability.

There will be time for you to do a short presentation after break. This should focus on teacher autonomy and how you are promoting this across the school.

I would also like to talk to some of the pupils and a few parents of my choice.

I expect the process to be finished by lunchtime.

I will let you know my decision by 4pm. I look forward to meeting you all.

Teacher

Learning Walk – Did the Teacher?

Dear Staff,

When I walked into your lessons...

- Was the learning objective shared?
- Was the learning objective discussed?
- Was the success criterion mentioned?
- Was the previous lesson referred back to?
- Did the TA look busy?
- Did the teacher involve the TA in the input?
- Did the lesson have pace?
- Did pupils engage with the resources positively?
- Were resources used correctly?
- Were pupils using the resources confidently?
- Were pupils discussing their learning?
- Were pupils listening without yawning?
- How often did the teacher use praise?
- How often did the pupils call out?
- How often did the TA ask for help?
- Were the more able stretched?
- Were the pupil premium pupils engaged?
- Were SEN pupils working independently?
- Were open-ended questions deployed appropriately?
- Was the overall level of challenge good enough?
- What was the balance between teacher talk and child talk?
- Were there opportunities for pupils to read out their work?
- Did the teacher use three mini plenaries?
- Did the teacher use a final plenary?
- Did the pupils enter the classroom silently?
- Did all the pupils sit down quickly?
- How well did the pupils line up?
- How many pupils were whispering?
- Was mastery taking place?
- Was there time for purple pen work?

- Was there good use of IT?
- Were tables set out in rows?
- Had all eight display boards been updated recently?
- Did displays have pupils work up?
- Did displays have questions on?
- Had pupils responded to written feedback?
- Was all work marked? All.
- Were next steps shared?
- Was display text 50% handwritten?
- Did the teacher use lolly sticks?
- Did the teacher give up to 30 seconds for a pupil to answer a question?
- Did accelerated learning take place?
- Did pupils know what they were learning?
- Could pupils regurgitate the learning objective and explain in great detail how to achieve it?
- Did the teacher make good use of talk buddies?
- Did the classroom have a reading corner?
- Did the classroom have the school motto up in the room?
- Was there a positive mind-set quote anywhere?
- Had the teacher written the date neatly?
- Was the date straight?
- Did the teacher make good use of the working walls?
- Did the teacher update the working walls during lesson?
- How often did pupils call out?
- How did the teacher respond to low level disruption?
- Was there evidence of assessment for learning from the previous lesson?
- How did the teacher use assessment for learning in the lesson?
- Did any pupils look out of the window? Even for a couple of seconds?
- Did the pupils enjoy the lesson?
- How did the teacher give feedback from the previous lesson?
- How did the teacher move around the classroom?
- How quickly did the teacher address misconceptions?

- How did the teacher talk to the pupils?
- Did the teacher invite pupils up to use the IWB?
- Were any pupils using the classroom computers?
- Was the teacher wearing their name badge?
- Was there evidence that the teacher was using a safety mug for their tea?
- How tidy was the classroom?
- Were all pupils challenged?
- Were all pupils looking at the teacher?
- Did the teacher stay positive?
- Did the teacher remain calm when being observed?
- Did the teacher pull a one-off lesson out of the bag?
- Was the lesson a typical lesson by teacher?
- Is the teacher on UPS?

Can I use elements of the lesson to put the teacher on an action plan?

Probably. Should be quite straight forward.

Teach Primary Article
NQT Year

Dear Newly Qualified Teachers,

Congratulations on your new job!

You won't be that boring teacher you remember at school. *You'll* be different. Your methods will be hip and trendy. You'll think outside the box and spend hours creating innovative and engaging lessons.

Perhaps the TV adverts attracted you to the role? After all, they promised inflated salaries, and suggested that the five children in your class will be impeccably behaved. They showed that lessons are fun and the rapport between the teacher and pupils as excellent. Perhaps they motivated you to want to plan original and interesting lessons for your new class?

You probably already have lots of great ideas for your display boards that will enthuse learning and are looking forward to marking work in a way you feel, will motivate pupils to feel good about their efforts. You probably have exciting, fresh new topics that you want to introduce too.

You must be very excited, because after all your training and hard work, you'll soon be allowed to teach and nurture your very own class. The feeling is almost overwhelming, but the responsibility of choosing what and how to teach is what makes the job so rewarding.

Maybe that's why you became a teacher.

Now for a reality check.

Due to my incessant drive for consistency, I will tell you *exactly* what to do.

Topics:

These are already planned for you. The senior leadership team have spent hours writing long-term plans. You may find them uninspiring, as they do drag on a bit. But you can't change them. Sorry.

English:

You must not deviate from our strict six-week rolling program. We have already decided the genres you will teach because it must fit into our long-term plan. Learning journeys in books must show good progress for Ofsted, so don't dip into random writing lessons in response to local news or unusual events. It makes the books look disjointed.

I have selected books from a reading spine list for whole-class texts. I have allocated you six books to read to the class. You are not allowed to read any of your favourite books because they might not be 'quality texts'. Please don't deviate from the list even if the books on it provide little inspiration.

Maths:

Maths must be taught using the scheme we bought. Not everyone likes it, but you'll need to follow it to the letter. Also, you must use the resources and textbooks that accompany the maths scheme – we spent a lot of money on them. Do not deviate from the scheme even if you don't like the lessons.

Displays:

Every class has been given the same six display boards covering set subjects. Use these. You don't have a choice. I'll carry out learning walks to ensure my display policy is followed. I will even tell you what colours to use and how to mount work.

Marking:

I use a five-page book scrutiny checklist to ensure conformity. You will use certain coloured highlighters, pens and stampers. You will be expected to type up and print learning objectives for every lesson. Children are not allowed to write their own titles (saving you hours of time each week).

When you talk to a child, I will expect a verbal feedback stamper to be used to prove you spoke to them. Most of how and what you mark isn't for the pupils anyway – it's for observers, and to satisfy my obsession for consistency. I will scrutinise your books regularly and give *you* written feedback.

Data:

I will meet up with you every half-term to ensure all children are making excellent progress. If they are not making accelerated progress, I will put pressure on you to ensure they catch up in afternoon intervention groups. Sadly, they will miss out on the wider curriculum you know they enjoy.

Even though I dictate how I want things done, you'll be held fully accountable for your class data. In addition, please ensure you have evidence of any professional judgements you make (e.g. film a child counting in 4s or write down everything children say in guided reading instead of actively and attentively listening to them). I have a problem with trust.

Finally, you'll be exhausted after the first few weeks because I'll expect you to be as good as an experienced teacher from day one. Your data and books will need to look identical to theirs. It's all about consistency. Everyone must be the same. I can't afford for Ofsted to pick up on any inconsistencies in data.

After a while, you'll find working 50-60 hours a week a strain on your friendships, relationships and general well-being.

I will do my best to ensure you get the non-contact time you're supposed to receive, but I can't promise.

Good luck,

Fake Headteacher

Teach Primary Article
Next Steps and Coloured Highlighters

Head: The progress your class is making in writing is very good. Well done. However, please make sure you write more feedback in their books. We must play the game.

Teacher: Thank you noticing the progress the class are making. They are responding well to my feedback.

Head: I just think you could make the advice you give more obvious. If someone looks through your books, there isn't enough teacher feedback evident.

Teacher: I don't understand. What do you mean? I give so much feedback and advice in every lesson.

Head: Our new non-negotiables list was discussed in the staff meeting. I expect you to follow it.

Teacher: I do try, but if I've already given feedback to the child, I don't write it down in their book. It's not for the pupil, is it?

Head: I understand, but I do expect you to write down next steps every lesson and to use your green and pink highlighter to show the parts you liked and the parts that need improving.

Teacher: But you said my class were making very good progress. Writing out *one* 'next step' per pupil, when I have given them *10* pieces of feedback already in the lesson, seems pointless. Is that what you mean by 'playing the game?'

Head: Yes. It's all about the books. We have to be seen to be improving the children's work. If we double our efforts and write more feedback on their work, it will look really good.

Teacher: But when you observed me the other day, you wrote, 'You made good use of praise for quality sentences and modelled sentences orally and by writing them on the board. You challenged children by focusing on vocabulary and grammatical features and encouraged them to improve sentences in a variety of ways. You quickly picked up on common errors and addressed them in lesson and gave particular extensions to more able writers.'

'You stopped the class several times to remind them of the correct use of semicolons and noticed children who were struggling and intervened quickly. You made good use of your TA who was focusing on handwriting and challenged and praised pupils throughout. You created a class toolkit of how to write well and reviewed this throughout the lesson. You asked lots of open-ended questions.'

Head: But it's all about the books.

Teacher: After my lessons, I always flick though the books and make decisions about my next lesson. If I notice that lots of pupils have made similar errors, I might address this as a whole class.

Often, I'll ask my TA to work with a small group the next day (or the same day if appropriate) to address a particular weakness. There's no need for me to write a 'next step' in their book when it's the next lesson. I give so much feedback in class. If children have done everything I've asked of them (and more, in most cases), I will praise them for it. To write next steps all the time so we can *prove* our impact will only annoy pupils. They'll think, 'I do everything you ask but you still tell me it's not quite right.'

Head: I understand all of that. But we have so many external visitors now who demand to look at books. It just looks really good if we write lots of next steps and use coloured highlighters and pens.

Teacher: But shouldn't progress in books be the only thing they look at? So much hidden feedback occurs in every lesson. Why must only *one* piece of feedback be written down, rather than all the feedback?

Head: Don't be daft. That would take too long.

Teacher: So, writing *one* next step is simply 'playing the game'?

Head: Yes. I've already said that. Listen, it's all about consistency. You are clearly a great teacher, but I must ensure members of staff are following my rules. It is what it is.

Teach Primary Article
Working Walls

I first encountered working walls about five years ago. The Head at the time had heard about them being used in a local school and decided our school should use them too. He didn't want to be left behind with the latest fad.

Overnight, our displays were deemed inadequate. He started the staff meeting with the words 'I am disappointed with the displays in the classroom and don't feel pupils are learning anything from them.'

As you can imagine, staff were bemused. All the classrooms looked amazing and stunning. Displays were changed every term (all 6 in every class) and were all very personal to each teacher and class.

Overnight, without warning, our displays were now useless. He continued by taking us to see a classroom with working wall displays in place. The deputy's class had been transformed (overnight?) – now a modelled classroom full of working walls. He claimed that her working walls had been helping the children make excellent progress. We knew the displays were new and this was another game-playing exercise.

By the end of the week, all the classrooms had to adopt the new working wall model. They had to be based on the working walls we were shown.

- Nothing mounted
- Paper pinned up at funny angles
- Paper overlapping the borders
- Everything handwritten
- Updated daily

They had to look raw and edgy. We were told that each working wall had to make it obvious what the pupils were learning so an observer could quickly see what the class had been working on.

Now the penny dropped. So, it was more to do with providing evidence of the learning that was taking place and nothing to do with the actual learning? Of course, the Head disagreed. Working walls were now part of the school's non-negotiable list.

We had to have working walls for writing, maths, science, spelling and topic. They had to be updated every lesson and everything had to be taken down and started again every 1-3 weeks.

Most of the time, boards were half empty and looked messy. They were often out of date because the teachers couldn't find time to update them. But he liked messy. It showed (proved) how current and trendy the working walls were. He claimed that children use them to aid their learning. We disagreed.

Where was the evidence that a static display affected children's learning? Where was the evidence that working walls made a difference to learning? Was he aware of the work involved in maintaining working walls?

We argued that updating so many display boards added to our workload and, contrary to what he thought, pupils didn't use the working walls to help them.

Telling staff what displays we had to create, how often to change them and what they needed to look like, demotivated us further. We enjoyed having complete autonomy over our classrooms. Now that was gone.

Most teachers I speak to don't want to be told how to use their display boards in their classrooms. Standing in the middle of an empty classroom and pondering over how to transform it into an engaging and inspiring place to work in, is all part of the fun of being a teacher.

I recently put up a display called the 'Proud Wall'. Every child had a space for them to put up some work they were proud of. The pupils loved it. It had all sorts of work on it: maths, writing, art, science, topic etc. I was told that having pupils' work on display doesn't do anything to help pupils learn. I was quickly told to take it down because it wasn't a working wall. The wall had to be empty when the pupils walked in on the first day of term so I could put things up on the working wall over the next few weeks.

My spelling display was interactive - full of activities the children could engage with. But it wasn't a working wall, so I had to take it down. The spelling working wall had to have that week's spelling on and nothing else. It had to make it very clear to visitors what the learning was. Ironically, the children lost all interest in the display but at least I ticked a box.

In some years, I have asked the class to help choose what the display boards should have on them. It is their classroom after all. When was the last time we asked children what they would like on their display boards?

If the teacher doesn't own their classroom, they don't fully invest in it. Imagine being a pupil going through primary school where the displays always look the same. Consistency isn't always the answer.

Teach Primary Article
Teacher Retention

Over the last five years I have seen excellent, experienced teachers leave the profession. Many who haven't left, regularly talk about how to leave. Those who can't leave, complain about their job. If this doesn't apply to you, thank goodness!

I have seen brilliant teachers have long periods of sick leave due to stress and anxiety. I have seen caring Headteachers develop health problems because the job has evolved in a manner they struggle to sustain.

In fact, in the last three schools I have worked in, more teachers were complaining and grumbling about the job than ever before. When I started teaching twenty years ago, I can't remember anyone moaning about their job. Everyone was happy and work life balance was good. We regularly met up socially and the atmosphere in school was positive.

I have been clinging on by my fingertips myself in recent years. Sadly, a new breed 'super Head' started at one of my previous schools, sending most staff into a spiral of depression and anxiety. I define these 'super Heads' as Headteachers who are only interested in improving data and exam results (and how to do this whatever it takes!). They bring with them a long list of demands, non-negotiables and pages of 'conformity' lists to adhere to.

Luckily, my new Headteacher at my new school is fantastic and has very sensible, manageable policies (and it's a requires improvement school). If it wasn't for this recent experience, and restored faith in his good leadership style, I have no doubt I too, would have left teaching.

So, what's changed since I started teaching?

Non-negotiables are probably one of the most damaging aspects of current management styles. In order for a Head to prove their impact on the school, they introduce pages of non-negotiables that they check you are implementing on a regular basis. Followers of Fake Headteacher regularly send me examples of their long list of 'conformance' tick sheets.

In one school, the new 'super Head' introduced a twenty-point tick list that all staff had to show evidence of during three unannounced learning walks – all within one half-term. The staff were told, if they failed to hit all twenty items on the list, they would be put on a coaching program. The unions were heavily involved.

I have personally experienced a 'super Head' who told us all we had to use his new planning sheet that involved having three learning objectives that you shared with three separate groups. He banned whole class teaching inputs. He said that any whole class input would either be too easy or too hard for some of the children. We were told we had to split off into groups immediately, so the learning was always directed at the correct level. The teaching assistant had to teach a group and stay put.

When most of us found it hard to implement, coaching programs were set up and some were threatened with capabilities.

Learning walks. Where did they spring up from? I understand the rationale behind them but more often than not, they are simply used as a way of policing the long list of non-negotiables. I can't remember the last time a teacher said, 'Thank you so much for popping into my class and appreciating what I do. The positive comments you made were lovely.'

If the 'super Head' sees something they don't like during their ten-minute visit, you are told off and more likely to suffer more visits to check you are doing everything right.

Book scrutinies. 'It's all about the books people.' Again, teachers are spending more time ensuring they have included the long list of things are stuck in or written in books. When was the last time your book scrutiny feedback started with, 'Amazing progress from the pupils. Well done. Your teaching has obviously had a positive effect on the class.'?

Progress in books seems to be low priority in my experience. LOs stuck in? Date written? Feedback given three times a week? Peer feedback given? Evidence of purple pen used? Highlighters used? Feedback stampers used? Use of verbal feedback stamper evident etc…

Teacher autonomy and trust has almost disappeared. Until Headteachers fully commit to improving this, I worry that many good teachers will continue to leave.

Teach Primary Article
Progress

The first school I worked in was a two-form entry junior school. Nearly all parents attended parents' evenings and regularly read with their children. They took an active role with homework and supported the teachers positively.

The children were mostly emotionally literate and able to work and socialise with each other well. It was an over-subscribed school. As a result, it could afford to pay for extra teaching assistants.

Due to lack of sleep (I had a new-born baby) I played it safe when Ofsted arrived, bumbling my way through a maths lesson that I knew all the children could do. My pupils behaved impeccably as usual.

I was expecting the inspector to rip the lesson apart. When I went for my feedback, I was surprised when he said it was one of the best lessons he'd seen.

He said, 'You had the children eating out of the palm of your hand. Your classroom management was wonderful, and the atmosphere was very positive. The children loved the work and you have a fantastic relationship with them. It was outstanding.'

It wasn't a good lesson – let alone an outstanding one, but because our Year 6 results had been good for several years, the school was graded good with many outstanding features.

For family reasons, I soon decided to move to a school much closer to home. I found one I really liked – a one form entry primary.

I thought the Headteacher was fantastic and very honest about the children. 'Most classes have a high number of social and emotional needs,' she informed me.

'A lot of parents don't help with homework and rarely listen to their children read. Several children often need restraining. Drug and alcohol use have become issues with some families.'

She continued, 'The children struggle to socialise positively despite the many social programs and whole school initiatives that we're running. Due to financial reasons, we can't afford as many teaching assistants as we'd like, but you'll get one three times a week for two hours.'

I accepted the challenge and was offered the job.

My first term there was a real eye-opener. I spent many evenings working very late into the night trying to plan lessons that would support the many needs of the class.

It was incredibly hard but extremely rewarding. The staff there were amazing.

Eventually, after a lot of hard work and effort, Max had stopped throwing chairs. Ryan and Abbie learnt not to shout at each other. Only a handful of children now fell out at lunchtime.

No longer did pupils say, 'I can't do it – I'm so rubbish.' Jack and Leo had developed strategies so they could stay in their seats rather than hiding under the table. Jessica wasn't throwing pencil pots anymore.

Due to the hard work of staff and my efforts to adapt to the daily needs of the class, they all began to make good progress, socially and emotionally.

After a while they seemed like a different class. Yes, we had a long way to go and some days were not great, but overall, the children were progressing.

When Ofsted paid us a visit the inspector said, 'You didn't stretch the more able. The less able were too reliant on concrete approaches. Children called out rather than putting up their hand. It was a little noisy at times and their handwriting was poor.'

I felt so disappointed. How could she not understand? The fact that they had even done *some* work – and felt proud of it – was massive progress.

Year 6 results at this school were never particularly good, but the Head's priorities were very different to those of my previous Head. We were given a 'requires improvement' grading and morale slumped.

Staff left or had breakdowns due to the excessive workload that followed. It was a shame Ofsted didn't see the important steps being made. Progress takes many forms.

Sadly, it seems, progress in the form of end-of-Key-Stage results is the only one that is looked at seriously and this puts many schools at a disadvantage.

Teach Primary Article
Non-negotiables

I am sitting in the primary staff room four weeks into the new academic year. I should feel rested, reinvigorated and bursting with excitement for the year ahead, but I don't. I haven't done for a few years now.

It's an odd feeling, because I have always loved my job. I look around and I can see the same confused expressions imprinted on the faces of my colleagues.

Soon, someone utters the words, 'But I don't understand why we are doing it'. Another says, 'It's too much work,' followed by, 'It's not for me or the children.'

Five minutes before lunch ends, everyone slumps back in their chairs and says, 'Do we have to go back to class?'

I remember saying to my parents, a few years into my teaching career, 'I am so lucky. It doesn't even feel like going to work. I love it.' Lately, I try not to talk about teaching with my parents as I get cross, which leaves them worrying about my well-being.

So, what's changed? I started looking back at a time when I felt most happy teaching. What was it that made the job so rewarding?

Here's my list: I felt trusted, I had a lot of autonomy, how my exercise books looked was up to me, I had a good work-life balance, I enjoyed taking clubs, nobody moaned in the staffroom, data was collected through an assessment week in May.

Yes, the job was hard, but it was an amazing feeling to be fully responsible for the education of my class, pinching ideas from the experienced teachers around me and having the freedom to try out and develop my own methods without fear or excessive scrutiny.

We were encouraged to team teach and pop in to watch colleagues. We were never told how to do our jobs. That's what our training was for.

I then tried to pinpoint why I now feel so fed up and disillusioned. Again, another list: I don't feel trusted, I don't have autonomy, I am told exactly how exercise books should look, I work most evenings just to keep up, I resent taking clubs because of my workload, morale is low in the staffroom, data is collected all the time and evidence is needed to support it.

Many of us must adhere to a lengthy book scrutiny checklist.

For example, learning objectives have to be typed up, a success criterion should be evident, two stars and a wish every day, deep mark once a week, use pink and green highlighters, use purple pens for editing, stamp this, annotate that, pupil voice, peer feedback, responding to marking, initialling every piece of work, and so on. It's so confusing.

To make things worse, many schools now have a long list of non-negotiables you have to follow, telling you how to teach, what your displays should look like, what resources you have to use, how the 'golden thread of learning' should appear in your books, etc.

Staff at my current school are always asking each other, 'What else do we need to do again?' After walking into another class and seeing the teacher sticking something in the books, they'll say, 'I forgot we had to do that.'

Of course, it should always be about progress over time. Would my class make progress even if I didn't mark my books or type up a learning objective? Yes, they would, because I know, on a daily basis, who needs further support or extending for a particular lesson and plan accordingly. Teach, review, feedback, plan. It's a very basic principle of teaching.

We work so hard satisfying book scrutiny checklists and non-negotiables that it feels like we are wearing straitjackets. Every half-term, I receive written feedback about my books. There's always room for improvement and notes about not having evidence for this or that. Checking for progress over time seems to be very low on the list these days.

I know eight experienced teachers who have left teaching in the last two years. They loved the job but couldn't stand how micro-managed the profession had become.

Fortunately, I have heard of some schools that are beginning to address the problem - moving away from written marking policies to feedback policies, for example. I fear that many more experienced teachers will leave the profession unless something is done about the excessive scrutiny and micro-management of staff.

At the moment, I wouldn't hesitate to leave if I could afford to. I never thought I would ever say that. It's sad.

Teach Primary Article
Academy Workload

Recently I started teaching in a school where the Head had a proven track record for nurturing challenging and deprived children and made them feel confident and leaving school with a love for learning. It was a school where staff refused to spend all of Year 6 rehearsing SATs papers and spent every afternoon clinging onto the wider curriculum.

The large academy that took over the same year, suddenly sacked the Head. Everyone was shocked. The staff felt deflated, the pupils were upset, and the parents were extremely confused. There wasn't even an opportunity for the Head to say goodbye after ten years at the school. Apparently, the Year 6 SATs results were not high enough.

A new Head was appointed. She had to prove her impact - quickly. She observed everyone in her first week. The majority of teachers were judged inadequate despite having a history of good or outstanding teaching at several other schools. The academy was happy. She had identified the problem. She soon sent everyone to other schools in the academy to observe teachers teaching the 'academy way'. It felt like a tick box strategy to show how she was helping to improve the school.

Later that term, she instructed us that all lessons must be typed up the night before using her new A4 format. Every lesson had to have three objectives to meet the needs of the class. A long list of non-negotiables was also introduced – from typing up daily learning objective slips to the use of coloured pens and highlighters and daily next steps written in books.

Everyone was soon struggling to keep up with the workload. It was not uncommon for staff to be working sixty-hour weeks to keep on top of the new demands. The Head said by Christmas, 25% of us would be good teachers again because she had written this on her action plan.

She was particularly pleased with one teacher who was soon asked to teach Year 6. The teacher was told that she was ideal for the role because of her experience, hard work and ability to form strong relationships with the pupils. The new teacher in Year 6 was soon doing a great job. The pupils were making excellent progress.

Then HMI visited the school and informed the Head that the teaching in Year 6 was not good enough without seeing any Year 6 lessons. Staff were confused as the report was obviously based on historic data and nothing to do with the current teacher.

The Year 6 teacher was called immediately into the Head's office where she was put on a coaching program. The Head said she felt 'vulnerable'. She knew her job was on the line. The teacher was understandably shocked and upset. She had been told her lessons were buzzing by the Head just a few days before.

The Year 6 teacher soon spent every night working to midnight trying to satisfy the new demands being placed on her. But it was no good. It didn't matter what she did, it wasn't good enough. She was soon threatened with capabilities. She found it hard to sleep because she was so anxious. Staff members rallied around her and told her she was being bullied and the Head was panicking. They told the teacher that the Head should have defended her. 'But what if the SATs are poor again and the academy hasn't taken action on based on the HMI report?' said some. 'The teacher is being set up to fail,' said others.

The teacher was signed off for two weeks with stress. Upon her return, she was told she was no longer required to teach Year 6 and told to teach Reception. Staff were horrified as they soon realised, they could be next.

The parents in Year 6 were angry as they had a strong relationship with the teacher and demanded a meeting with the Head. She refused to tell them why the teacher had been removed prompting comments from one parent that the teacher must have done something 'very bad' to be suddenly removed like that.

The teacher resigned and found another job within weeks. Although it took the teacher nearly two years to recover, she successfully became part of the SLT team at her new school where she continues to make a positive impact. Since the academy took over, ten teachers have resigned. It is a one form entry school.

The Year 6 did well that year. The academy told pupils they had to attend early morning and after school booster groups and paid for a company to run booster lessons every day in school. The wider curriculum was abandoned until after the SATs.

Because of their improved SATs results, they are now a good school.

A good school?

Teach Primary Article
Ofsted Isn't the Problem

Ofsted must exist. There must be spot checks carried out in schools in order to protect children and to encourage improvement and recognise success.

Yes, Ofsted can improve. Yes, they are beginning to listen to school leaders. Yes, they are regularly looking at ways to make the process fairer and less threatening.

I have experienced eight Ofsted inspections in various schools. I have fully experienced the emotions involved when receiving the Ofsted result. Good and bad.

I have worked for nine Headteachers: all of them, very different in their approach. I have worked in good schools where the atmosphere was dreadful. I have worked in requires improvement schools where the atmosphere was extremely positive. I know teachers in outstanding schools who hate their job.

Teacher retention has very little to do with your school's Ofsted grade. It has everything to do with how your school is managed and how the Head copes with the pressures to improve the school.

My summary of how three particular Heads managed their school:

School A: Requires Improvement

'I will improve this school by introducing non-negotiables that suffocate teacher autonomy. I will carry out excessive book looks and learning walks. I will put teachers on support plans over the slightest imperfections. I will tell staff what to put up on display boards and how they should be presented. I will regularly test children for data purposes. I won't invest in teacher well-being or fully understand the pressures involved teaching in this particular catchment area. Year 6 pupils will spend the year in booster groups at the expense of the wider curriculum. I will do whatever it takes to get a good Ofsted grade.'

Result: The atmosphere at school was awful. Very good teachers left. Long term sickness was an issue. Because the SATs results improved, the school was later judged good. It was not a good school.

School B: Requires Improvement

'I will improve this school by reading literature on educational research. I will improve this school by refusing to carry out booster groups all year for Year 6. I will regularly address and discuss workload with staff and try, where possible, to cut down on non-negotiables that are not in the pupils or teachers' interest. I will insist that the arts have priority in the school and stop the obsession with literacy and maths. I won't put staff on support plans just because their data isn't great. I will praise staff for their efforts. I will give back autonomy to teachers wherever possible. I want to treat staff professionally and fully trust them to do their job.

Result: The atmosphere was great. Staff were happy most of the time. Long term sickness was non-existent. SATs results were average to good. The school was judged good. It was a good school. Pupils were happy. Teachers had job satisfaction.

School C: Good

'I want more. I want his school to be outstanding. I have no family and school is my life. I will do anything to get the recognition I crave. I am obsessed with getting this school to outstanding. I will make staff work so hard and make them feel guilty for not giving up enough of their own time. I will off-roll pupils who will affect our SATs data and make it extremely difficult for pupils with special needs to enrol. SATs boosters will be standard from Year 4. I will make friends in all the right places and invite important people to the school to show off my efforts.'

Result: School life was the only thing the Head knew. She had no family of her own. Unfortunately, she didn't realise many teachers did have families and needed a good work life balance. The children were well behaved so teachers were reluctant to leave as they had heard some horror stories at other schools. Staff retention was good, but they were on their knees. The pressure to improve was constant and excessive. The school was graded outstanding. It wasn't outstanding. It was an illusion. The Head became an academy chain director earning big money and was soon implementing her policies at lots of schools.

Your Ofsted grade does not affect teacher well-being and overall job satisfaction.

Teacher well-being and job satisfaction is absolutely affected by how your Headteacher decides to manage the school.

There. Said it.

Teach Primary Article
Formal Testing

When I started teaching, I remember the Head asking the class to complete a maths and reading test. The class did them. I marked them and handed the scores in. That was it. There was no scrutiny of my teaching, no target setting in pupil progress meetings and no talk of freezing my pay.

Over the years, the annual test turned into two tests a year. Then a test week was introduced once a term. And for some, you may even have a test week every half-term now.

At my next school, we had two test weeks a year. My first set of results were not great. I was called into the Head's office and given a good ticking off. He pointed out that my colleague, who was in the same year group, had excellent results.

After the meeting, I was confidentially told by another teacher, that my colleague had taught that year group for years and knew the tests inside out and knew how to play the game.

I was shocked but it helped explain the differences between the two classes. I went back through the papers and realised that lots of questions were based on content we hadn't even taught. My test results improved dramatically later on in the year! I felt bad but the Head was much happier.

When I moved schools again, the first thing I did was to look through the forthcoming test papers. I drip fed the questions into lessons and my results improved. Unfortunately for me, no one else did this and my results stuck out like a sore thumb. I was called into the Head's office and asked to bring my books to show evidence of progress. It was awkward. I vowed never to do it again.

But then I got cross. I realised that lots of questions in the test had nothing to do with what the pupils had been learning. What sort of testing system tests children on things you haven't yet taught? I challenged my next Headteacher about it. He said, 'I appreciate your concerns and it is a bit unfair, but it does provide us with important data throughout the year.'

Having spoken to a few friends about this issue, they have admitted doing things such as: 'giving children extra time than the test states to complete it, reading out questions to the whole class to make sure they understand, pointing out errors on papers as they walk by, carrying out warm up problems / questions before the test to ensure those questions are completed correctly, giving back papers to pupils if they should have done better.' etc.

Recently, a deputy Head, who I was good friends with at the time, said the Head knew this sort of thing happened but the 'data looks good and keeps Ofsted off our back.'

This annoyed me further.

The tests are often so different to what happens in class. In what maths lesson would I expect children to answer 30-40 questions based on random mathematical knowledge from 2 step fraction problems to reading a 24-hour train timetable - all within 45 minutes. Typically, the pupil might answer a handful of questions in a lesson, but all based on the same skill. No wonder Year 4 pupils fall apart when they see the test.

In what reading lesson would I expect children to answer 30-40 questions based on three different text types (that they haven't studied before), using test question language they don't hear when discussing a class book. When would I expect my class to read and answer questions independently for 45 minutes when their normal reading lessons are only 20-30 minutes? The test doesn't test what I have taught and is completely different to what they've been exposed to.

I asked the Head if we could at least study the three text types in the term, so the children had seen them before - or even drip feed the types of reading questions they are expected to answer in lessons. He said no, as this would give an 'unfair advantage to the pupils'.

So, I continued to give the class long tests based on many things they hadn't been exposed to before. And to make things worse, the data is now often used to bash teachers over the head with.

Maybe we should stop testing in this manner.

Right, I'm off to take my piano exam. I just hope the examiner doesn't ask me to play pieces my teacher hasn't taught me yet!

Teach Primary Article
Leaving Teaching

I started teaching in 1997. I worked in a challenging area with amazing teachers who cared passionately about their job and the welfare and academic progress of the children. I stayed there for five years. They were the best five years of my teaching career.

I have just resigned from teaching after twenty-two years in the classroom. I didn't want to leave the best job in the world, but I had to.

So, what has changed since 1997?

There was still planning to be done, meetings to attend, clubs to run, displays to put up, marking to complete, concerts and shows to organise etc.

But that's what I do now. So, what's changed?

There was no official performance management back then. Well, there was. It was a very informal chat with the Headteacher about how my year had gone. It was heavily focused on my relationship with the class. He told me what he was pleased with and suggested some areas I might want to develop. It lasted twenty minutes over a nice cup of tea.

Now, performance management means: data, targets, pay review, progress and subject leadership amongst other things. I dread them. There's rarely a mention of the relationships I have worked so hard to form with my class and a lack of appreciation of the extra hours I put in at home to satisfy my workload.

Perhaps it's this that's changed?

Back then, staff weren't observed formally. You were just left to it but had the support and challenge from your peers. The Head would pop in now and again but often just to give you a message. He would smile and pick up on something positive the class were doing. He certainly didn't bring a notepad and make detailed notes on what I was doing or saying. Learning walks. What were they? They didn't exist. I didn't realise at the time, but I was being left to teach without criticism or judgement. It was lovely.

Now, I expect to endure 12 learning walks a year – each with written feedback. The feedback will focus what non-negotiables or whole school targets I had missed, or that my displays weren't quite right, or that my teaching slides weren't the correct colour. I am held account for anything that's not quite right. There is little trust and it's all about conformance not autonomy. All my enthusiasm and decision making about how I want to deliver lessons has gone. I am a robot, and I must do what I am told.

Perhaps it's this that's changed?

When I started teaching, I was in my early twenties. I could go out (yes, on a school night), and still have enough energy, enthusiasm and humour to deliver a great day for my class. I remember going to the pub with friends every night one week. I was young. It was great. I didn't have children of my own and regularly played sport.

Now, I have a family and going out every night is a distant memory. Even if I wanted to, I couldn't. I am tired! I am older. I don't have the same energy levels and enthusiasm for late nights. It doesn't seem to matter how early I go to bed or how many green teas I consume after midday, I am still tired (especially after lunch) and stare at envy at the teacher about to have their PPA. My energy levels are just not the same and when you are managing thirty primary children all day, this is not ideal.

Perhaps it's this that's changed?

My first teaching job was just this. It was my first proper job. Everything was an attack on the senses. It was brilliant and I felt very proud to be a teacher. I remember telling my parents how much I loved my job.

But of course, that was twenty-two years ago. Maybe this is it. Maybe I need a new challenge. I have seen fads come and go. I have seen teaching ideas come full circle. What was once frowned upon is now very cool. What is now frowned upon used to be very cool. Maybe I am just bored.

Perhaps it's this that's changed?

Whatever it is, I no longer have the desire to stay in teaching anymore. The passion has gone. I think I might be burnt out, but I don't really know for sure. All I know is how anxious and stressed I have become in recent years.

Teaching has changed.

www.headteacher-newsletter.com for 2020/21 blogs

Find Fake Headteacher on Twitter and Facebook

Find Fake Headteacher on Amazon

Search online for Teachwire and Teach Primary